© 2025 Deacon David Dufilho
All rights reserved.

ISBN 9798317224332

Published by St. Rose of Lima Catholic Church via Amazon Kindle Direct Publishing (KDP)

Amazon KDP website: https://kdp.amazon.com

Printed in United States

This is a work of non-fiction. Any resemblance to real persons, living or dead, is purely coincidental. No part of this book may be reproduced, stored in a retrieval system, or transmitted in any form or by any means, electronic, mechanical, photocopying, recording, or otherwise, without prior written permission of the publisher, except for the use of brief quotations in a book review or scholarly work.

Nihil obstat:

    University of St. Thomas at St. Mary's Seminary

    Theology Department, Houston Texas

Imprimatur:

    Daniel Cardinal DiNardo

    Apostolic Administrator of Galveston-Houston

    March 3, 2025

Discernment, Not Decisions

Navigating Life's Choices with Faith and Confidence

By: Deacon David Dufilho

Acknowledgements

Writing this book on discernment from a Catholic theological perspective came with more than a few challenges; challenges that I could not have faced on my own. In this regard, and from the bottom of my heart I would like to thank the clergy, staff, my friends and fellow parishioners of St. Rose of Lima in Houston Texas; it is a true blessing to be walking with each of you as we serve and grow closer to our Lord.

And to my friends on our Evangelization and Outreach team; first, to my friend and brother in Christ, Bao Huynh, thank you, without your leadership and guidance this book would not have been possible. Second to my team; Deacon Darryl Drenon, Gig Runge, Jeff Latcham, Heather Peterson, and Jackie Madden, what a gift from God to have all of you in my life. And we're just getting started!

And finally, to my proofreader; proofreader for the book, proofreader for my life, my wife Yira, I love you. Thank you for always standing by me as we continue our walk along this diaconate journey.

A Note

In the following chapters I share many experiences and stories. Whether personal stories or shared experiences, my intention was to bring a sense of realness to the book. And as my reflections and writing continued it was these personal stories and experiences that kept speaking to me. Although all true, where necessary and for confidentiality, I have changed most of the names.

Introduction

When approached to write this book, and in my discernment of asking am I supposed to write this book, my initial thought was ok I've discerned the diaconate, and yes, I do try to live a life of discernment. In all my ministry: From teaching OCIA to hospital ministry, from marriage preparation to preparing homilies, and everything else, I do try and discern what God wants me to do, but oh how many times have I faltered.

And the next thing that came to my mind was Vince Lombardi's quote, "It's not whether you get knocked down, it's whether you get up."

When we commit to a life of discernment, of praying God's will for us, of trying to see the Spirit in our day to day lives, we will experience moments of beauty, of goodness, of love. There will also be moments of frustration, we will make mistakes, and it will at times seem like we may lack the purity of heart to make right decisions.

Prayer, discernment of God's will, can at times seem baffling, confusing, mystifying, and it can seem like all of these and more because prayer is impossible to fully explain. Prayer is faith.

And that's precisely it: prayer is faith. Discernment of God's will for us is faith. When we turn to God in prayer, He remains mysterious, but slowly becomes approachable…even touchable. When we journey with Jesus, He slowly gives us a way we can learn to hear, and as we continue our journey, allows us to hear Him more and more closely.

As I wrote this book, I thought back to my days in diaconate formation. I thought about the many conversations I have had with parishioners, catechumens and candidates, friends and family, priests and fellow brother deacons on their prayer lives and discernments, on their journeys with their Maker. My intention is not at all to take you away from your personal way of discernment; rather my intention is more of a hope. And my hope is that these chapters encourage and nurture your journey…your life's journey of discerning God's will.

Table of Contents

Discernment, Not Decisions... 11
The Spiritual Foundation of Discernment.........................23
Recognizing God's Voice...39
The Role of Prayer in Discernment................................. 49
Discernment in Daily Life.. 64
Obstacles to Discernment.. 74
Spiritual Formation and Its Role
in Discernment..85
Cultivating a Discerning Heart.. 93
In Times of Uncertainty... 105
Spiritual Direction and Discernment...............................119
Discernment in Vocational
and Life Choices.. 131
The Fruit of Discernment: A Life
Aligned with God..143
Discernment as a Daily Practice...................................... 152
Living Out Discernment in Our World
…In God's World..161
An Invitation... 167

Chapter 1:

Discernment, Not Decisions

You are a Beloved Child of God

"First and foremost, you must know that you are truly a beloved daughter of God," I said to Margaret, who sitting next to me in our chapel one winter afternoon had just shared, "I want a better relationship with God…I want to do His will, but it feels like He's not listening to me…He isn't answering my prayers."

As a deacon, when I sit with someone young or old, knee-to-knee seeking advice, or in an OCIA class or marriage prep meeting, in my hospital ministry, in nearly all my preaching, I want to always extend this message:

You are a beloved child of God. You are a unique incarnation of God made in his image and likeness. As His child, your mission is to bring real and visible expressions of His presence to the people in your family and community, both to those you know and the strangers whose path you cross every day.

"How do I do that?" Margaret asked.

That is the question we all face at some point.

How do we find God's love within ourselves and then extend it to others? Is it as simple as deciding to love, or is there more to it? Why does it sometimes feel so difficult, even burdensome, to live this out? The reality is that God's love cannot be grasped by sheer willpower or a mere decision. His love is too big, too vast, too uncontainable, and so much more than we can express ourselves.

St. Paul tells us,

> *Do not conform yourselves to this age but be transformed by the renewal of your mind, that you may discern what is the will of God, what is good and pleasing and perfect.*

(Romans 12:2)

This scripture speaks to the heart of the matter. Living as a beloved child of God and reflecting His love in the world requires a transformation that begins in the mind and spirit. It is a continual process of becoming more aligned with God's desires for our lives.

As St. Paul reminds us, God's will is good, pleasing, and perfect. It is through discernment—the process of seeking God's will in our lives—that we learn to see the world, our actions, and our relationships through His eyes. Discernment involves taking time to listen to God's voice, understand His desires for us, and aligning our hearts with His.

We cannot merely decide to hold or share God's love with our own strength. God's love is far too vast and profound to be held just by deciding to do so. We cannot summon it at will; it must begin in love, be accepted, be received and then allowed to flow through us. His love is transformational, not transactional. We must allow God to love us fully, to fill us with His presence and grace; it is only then that we can go out and share His love with our neighbors, our communities, our world.

So, where do we go from here? How do you and I accept, give, and live out God's love in our world? The answer begins with surrender—surrendering ourselves to God's transformative love and allowing that love to change us. God's love is sacrificial love. Acceptance of God's love and living out His will can only be gained and shared through what we call Christian discernment.

It involves prayer, reflection, and a willingness to listen to God's voice through the Holy Spirit. Through this discernment process, we open ourselves to be vessels of His love, reflect His light in the world, and serve others as He has served us.

Living out God's love requires courage, vulnerability, and trust. It's not always easy, but if we stay the course, He will lead us down the most fulfilling and meaningful path.

As you and I reflect on our journey of discerning God's will and living as His beloved children, we begin to realize that the foundation of everything we do in this life is rooted in love—not just any love, but agape love—the selfless, unconditional love that God has for each of us. Through agape love, we understand God's heart and, in turn, our true mission in this world—to love as He has loved, to be His hands and feet in a world in desperate need of His grace.

In defining love, the Greeks distinguished four types:

1. **Philia**: The love of friendship and companionship. It involves mutual respect, shared values, and a deep bond between friends.
2. **Storge**: Familial love, the natural affection between parents and children or family members.
3. **Eros**: Romantic or passionate love, often associated with physical attraction and desire.
4. **Agape**: The highest form of love - selfless, unconditional love reflecting God's love for humanity. It is sacrificial with concern for the well-being of others.

God's love, this agape love, is a transformative love that moves us to live out God's will in our world. Only through Christian discernment can we fully embrace and then go out and share this love with others. When we encounter this love through the Holy Spirit, our actions, our lives and how we live them are transformed. It is by this love that we become sisters and brothers in Christ. This realization of our deepest desire, to love and be loved, moves us to bring Christ into the world in such a way that the incarnation is renewed. It is about making the Gospel alive in our own lives and in those with whom we share our lives.

So, what's next? How do we discover or rediscover what God has placed us on this earth to do?

How do we connect with our shared vocation in service to our hearts, our neighbors, and our communities?

How do we renew this Incarnation of Christ in our world today?

The answer is discernment. We must undergo the process of Christian discernment.

Christian discernment is different from decision making. Reaching a decision can be rather straightforward. We look at the question, challenge or goal before us, maybe get out a piece of paper and draw a line down the center of it, list the pros and cons of each possible choice, then choose the course that we feel will best meet our challenge. This process is often driven by immediate circumstances, practical concerns, and the desire for an efficient solution. We typically turn to our egos and rely heavily on our own reasoning, experiences, and sometimes intuition to determine what is most beneficial or appropriate.

Christian discernment takes the decision-making process to another level. It's not just about choosing between options based on logic or external outcomes—it's about seeking God's will amid uncertainty and complexity. Discernment is the spiritual practice of listening to God's voice and aligning our hearts with His desires. It requires patience, openness, and a willingness to go beyond the surface level of a situation. We must sit in God's silence and ask Him, "God here is what is going on, what do you think I should do...what do you want me to do?"

Christian discernment invites us to cultivate a posture of openness to the Holy Spirit, trusting that God will provide clarity over time as we remain faithful in our pursuit of His will—even when the path isn't clear, because often the path will not at all seem clear. And it is when we find ourselves on those cloudy, foggy, and even stormy paths, that it is only in discernment, when we let go of control, when we trust God and His timing, that we will truly know we are walking hand in hand with God.

As Franciscan friar and spiritual writer Richard Rohr explains, discernment is about something more profound. He cites Henri Nouwen's perspective:

Discernment... is about listening and responding to that place within us where our deepest desires align with God's desire. As discerning people, we sift through our impulses, motives, and options to discover which ones lead us closer to divine love and compassion for ourselves and others and which ones lead us further away. [1]

When we discern God's calling, we are met with one of three possible outcomes:

1. **We find our "True Self"** in discernment. We connect with our souls and recognize that God's genuine desire is our true desire. We know what we are meant to do, and we act.

2. **The answer is "No."** We may discover that God's answer is "No." In this case, we continue to draw closer to God, asking, "What is it that You desire for me, Lord?"

3. **The answer is "Not yet."** Sometimes, God says, "Slow down, enjoy the journey, and continue."

Discernment starts and ends through prayer and reflection, taking the time to reflect on our days and realize," Hey, that's what God was trying to tell me today," or "OK God this is what I'm hearing you say."

We may come to realize what previously seemed so important in our lives has lost much of its power over us. Our desire to be successful, wealthy, or popular becomes increasingly less important as we move closer to God's heart. We may even experience a strange inner freedom to follow a new call. A call that may have at first seemed to have come out of left field. As we pray more each day, as we come to know God and His will, and we experience His love, our world, and our purpose is gently made known to us. Our discernment will reveal new priorities, directions, and gifts given to us from God. [2] This is what happened to me as I discerned the diaconate; a formation and journey that continues to this day.

What else?

Discernment and what follows discernment is both joy and peace. When we truly realize that we are indeed a branch growing from the vine (John 15:4-5) much of our anxieties about worldly things dim, even vanish. We don't need to worry about what might happen. We don't have to agonize about tomorrow. We now understand that we are being guided by a loving hand. This understanding – that we are being guided-becomes our actual guidance. It is no longer about needing to fix it, or understand it, or manage it on our own. It is now about being able to trust, listen, and allow His desires to indeed become our desires. [3]

When we align our heart with God's heart, we know we are walking hand in hand with Him. We know what he wants us to do, what he wants us to work on, and even what he wants us to change or to fix in our world. We recognize that, as he sends us out, we are the hands and feet of Jesus.

A person living a life of discernment with God truly knows deeply that they are a beloved child of God. Being faith-filled, and living in and listening to their true self, they are used by God for bigger things.

Key Takeaways:

- **Understanding Our Identity as Beloved Children of God:** *"See what love the Father has bestowed on us, that we may be called the children of God. And that is what we are"* (1 John 3:1). What does it mean to be a beloved child of God, made in His image and likeness? Reflect on this truth: You are uniquely loved by God, and His love defines your identity. Embrace your role as His beloved child, understanding that you are created for a purpose, with infinite worth in His eyes.

- **Inviting the Holy Spirit to Align Your Heart with God's:** In your prayer time, do you invite the Holy Spirit to come into your heart? As you open your heart to Him, know that your God-Self, your soul, truly desires to be in union with God. Invite the Holy Spirit to guide you, to be with you, to draw you closer to God.

- **Finding Peace and Joy Through Discernment:** As you discern what God wants for you, you will be drawn closer to His will. It may feel intimidating at first, but trust that your anxieties will diminish as you listen attentively to the Spirit. Discernment brings clarity, and as you follow God's guidance, you will experience true joy and peace, knowing that you are walking in His purpose.

Sources
[1] Richard Rohr, *Discernment versus Decision Making*, Daily Meditations, Center for Action and Contemplation, May 31, 2018.
[2] Henri Nouwen, *Discernment: Reading the Signs of Daily Life* (Harper One: 2013), 17.
[3] Richard Rohr, *Discerning What is Ours to Do*, Daily Meditations, Center for Action and Contemplation, August 21, 2022.

Chapter 2:

The Spiritual Foundation of Discernment

Discernment in Scripture

As you and I journey towards becoming a discerning child of God, we can look to scripture for examples and advice. So, we begin by inviting the Holy Spirit to come into our hearts as we discern what a particular scripture might be trying to tell us. And as we open our bibles and look to scripture in our discerning prayer time, I think it is important to remember that you and I, we are not much different than the people we read about in the bible. Just as we go through our lives with our families, at work, at school… through all of life's ups and downs, so too did the people we read about in the bible.

Discernment, seeking God's guidance and wisdom, is woven throughout much of the bible. Both in the Old Testament and the New Testament we find all types of people who come to understand the importance of seeking God's guidance and wisdom. People who meet God, meet Jesus, and come to believe. It may, and often does prove to be difficult, they may question or push back as many of them indeed do, (as you and I have probably done), but they come to believe, and it is in their coming to believe that they grow to better know that deep place residing in them where their desires align with their Maker's.

In the Old Testament, Solomon who succeeded David as king, understanding his youth and inexperience, but also recognizing that he was a servant of God, asked:

> *Give your servant, therefore, a listening heart to judge your people and to distinguish between good and evil…The Lord was pleased by Solomon's request. So God said to him: Because you asked for this-you did not ask for a long life for yourself, nor for riches, nor for the life of your enemies-but you asked for discernment to know what is right-I do now as you request. I give you a heart so wise and discerning that there has never been anyone like you until now…*

(1 Kings 3:9-12)

Just as Solomon's discernment led him to a deeper connection with God and a greater understanding of his role, our pursuit of wisdom can similarly guide us. In a world filled with distractions and decisions, we too can seek wisdom from God to help us navigate the complexities of life. Solomon's beautiful prayer of asking for a listening heart teaches us that our desire for understanding can move us beyond solving problems to actively aligning our hearts with God's desires.

Later in the Old Testament, we read of the Blessings of Wisdom in the book of Proverbs. The author invites us to seek understanding actively, urging us to treasure wisdom as we would a hidden treasure and to approach God with a heart ready to receive His guidance:

> *My son, if you receive my words*

and treasure my commands,
Turning your ear to wisdom,
inclining your heart to understanding;
Yes, if you call for intelligence,
and to understanding raise your voice;
If you seek her like silver,
and like hidden treasures search her out,
Then will you understand the fear of the L<small>ORD</small>*;*
the knowledge of God you will find;

(Proverbs 2:1-5)

We read Solomon's prayer, we read the beautiful lines from the book of Proverbs, and in reflection on these passages, perhaps we can better ask: What wisdom am I seeking today? How might that wisdom help me discern God's will more clearly? And as we ask these questions, we begin to align ourselves more closely with God's plan and better position ourselves to receive His divine wisdom.

As we turn to the pages to the New Testament, we find St. Paul encouraging us to develop a discerning spirit which he ties to love and knowledge as he prays:

> *And this is my prayer: that your love may increase ever more and more in knowledge and every kind of perception, to discern what is of value, so that you may be pure and blameless for the day of Christ, filled with the fruit of righteousness that comes*

> *through Jesus Christ for the glory and praise of God.*
>
> (Philippians 1:9-11)

In another of his letters, Paul speaks of the Holy Spirit who resides in us and who gives us the ability to discern spiritual truths, he writes:

> *Now the natural person does not accept what pertains to the Spirit of God, for to him it is foolishness, and he cannot understand it, because it is judged spiritually. The spiritual person, however, can judge everything but is not subject to judgment by anyone.*
>
> (1 Corinthians 2: 14-15)

If you are wondering what St. Paul means by "natural person," he clarifies this in subsequent verses writing,

> *Brothers, I could not talk to you as spiritual people, but as fleshly people, as infants in Christ.*
>
> (1 Corinthians 3:1)

Through this, Paul encourages believers, encourages us, to grow in spiritual maturity, urging all to move beyond a superficial understanding of faith to a deeper Spirit-guided discernment that can transform lives.

And then, the Gospels

Throughout the Gospels, time and time again, page after page, we see Jesus in prayer, spending deep discerning time with His Father. We see it at an early age when a 12-year-old Jesus stays back at the temple in Jerusalem. When his mom and dad go back in search of him, they find him sitting in his Father's house.

> *"Son, why have you done this to us? Your father and I have been looking for you with great anxiety." And he said to them, "Why were you looking for me? Did you not know that I must be in my Father's house."*
>
> (Luke 2: 48-49)

When we hear of Jesus again, he is an adult, about 30 years old, and before beginning his ministry he spends 40 days in discernment being led by the Holy Spirit in the desert (Luke 4: 1-12). Early in his ministry after performing several miracles in Capernaum, he leaves and retreats to a deserted place to pray. (Mark 1:35) Just before choosing his 12 Apostles, we read of Jesus retrieving to the mountain to pray; to discern on the twelve he would select. (Luke 6: 12). Later in his ministry,

> *... he took Peter, John, and James and went up the mountain to pray. While he was praying his face*

> *changed in appearance and his clothing became dazzling white.*
>
> (Luke 9: 28-29)

…the transfiguration of Jesus standing before His Father! Late in his ministry, we learn that while Jesus was ministering in the temple area in Jerusalem during the days, he would retreat at nighttime to a place called the Mount of Olives, (Luke 21: 37-38) presumably alone and in discernment with His Father.

And then, Gethsemane…The Agony in the Garden. When recalling these Gospel readings, we tend to remember this is where Jesus went to pray before being arrested. We remember him taking his disciples with him and asking them to pray and to keep watch, but they could not stay awake, and then Judas and the crowd show up to arrest, and ultimately murder Jesus. (Matthew 26: 36-46, Mark 14: 32-42, Luke 22: 39-46)

But next we turn to the John's Gospel, where the disciples presumably hear Jesus praying what some refer to as his "high priestly prayer". And speaking to his Father, he intercedes for not only his present-day disciples, but for you and me, his future disciples:

> *I pray not only for them, but also for those who will believe in me through their word, so that they may all be one, as you, Father, are in me and I in you,*

that they also may be in us, that the world may believe that you sent me. And I have given them the glory you gave me so that they may be one, as we are one, I in them and you in me, that they may be brought to perfection as one, that the world may know that you sent me, and that you loved them even as you loved me...I made known to them your name and I will make it known, that the love with which you loved me may be in them and I in them.

(John 17: 20-26)

Remember this scene. Remind yourself often of this Gospel reading when you pray and as you discern; that Jesus Christ prayed for you in the garden.

That they also may be in us...that the love with which you loved me may be in them and I in them.

How awesome is that? How beautifully awesome is the fact that Jesus prayed for you, that Jesus has a plan for you, that Jesus longs to have your deepest desires align with his deepest desires!

The Catholic Church and Discernment

What is the will of God for me and my life? God what do you want me to do? God I'm not sure I should do this or that? How often have I asked these and similar questions? How often have I brought these questions to God? How often have I heard God's answer or how often have I been confident in God's answer?

To live a full meaningful, joyful and moral life, you and I must exercise reason and faith when making decisions; sometimes difficult, sometimes maybe even painful, always with a certain degree of challenge. Yes, sometimes we will feel uncertain about God's response. It is in these moments when discernment becomes essential as we sincerely try to align our hearts with His.

The Catholic Church teaches that, in all things, we should turn to the cardinal virtues—prudence, justice, fortitude, and temperance—to help us discern God's will. These virtues serve as a compass, helping us align our actions with God's desires. St. Augustine's writings further illustrate this, stating:

> *To live well is nothing other than to love God with all one's heart, with all one's soul, and with all one's efforts; from this, it comes about that love is kept whole and uncorrupted (through temperance). No misfortune can disturb it (and this is fortitude). It obeys only [God] (and this is justice), and is careful in discerning things, so as not to be surprised by deceit or trickery (and this is prudence).*

(CCC, 1809)

Discernment is a process, a journey requiring time, reflection and prayer. Even seemingly "small" decisions can take time. My pastor comes up to me and says, "David, I want you to consider teaching a confirmation class," or David, "I'd like you to consider chairing the spring festival," these requests, depending on everything else going on in my life, may take more time in discernment than one might initially think.

There are also times when we may be faced with a moral question. My boss may come up to me and ask me to do something that pushes the envelope on my Christian morals, and the Church tells us,

> *Man is sometimes confronted by situations that make moral judgments less assured and decisions difficult. But he must always seriously seek what is right and good and discern the will of God expressed in divine law.*
>
> (CCC, 1787)

And then there's the life questions. The bigger the question, the more time discernment is needed. Questions like, "God what am I supposed to do with my life," or "God, are you really calling me?" These "life" questions require a significant amount of time in discernment. It is in these times, often lengthy periods of time, that God does reveal His will. It is in these times that God confirms his calling to us for the life he desires us to live.

For weeks, months, even years, in my daily visits with God, as I walk with Jesus and guided by the Holy Spirit I have an ongoing conversation: I talk to God openly asking am I open to respond to whatever call He has for me? Where is my heart in all of this? Does the thought of this possible calling give me hope, peace, even joy? Is my motivation one of selflessness, one of truly loving God, his people, and truly desiring to do what He wants me to do? I ask, I ponder, and I pray, "Lord, is this journey I'm contemplating, have you placed this on my heart, is this truly how I am to serve you?" These are serious questions, requiring dedicated time and devotion, as I grow in my relationship to God and truly discover my calling.

Discernment and Spiritual Growth

No two individuals's prayer life, spiritual growth and spiritual journey are alike: each being beautifully unique with its own divine thumbprint. As we grow and discern in our prayer life we talk to God, we read and meditate on scripture inviting the Holy Spirit into our hearts, and we devote time to visiting with Jesus, and as we do this, and as we grow in prayer, we begin to notice things in our everyday lives.

As we go about our day, we realize that the Holy Spirit is there with us, and He is constantly whispering to us the words of Jesus. We are each a unique puzzle piece to God's creation, and the Holy Spirit reveals our role in God's creation to us slowly, step by step. We come to understand

God's desire for us, our calling, through prayer, meditating on scripture, following the teachings of the Church, participating in the sacraments, and listening to the Holy Spirit; all of these relate to and are necessary for our Christian discernment.

And a note of caution; in our discernment we must make sure that our inspirations are indeed coming from God and are not coming from the spirit of the flesh, from the world or from the evil one. Remember our Triune God will never ask us to do anything the Church would consider immoral. The flesh, the world, and the evil one have a way of making something immoral seem enticing…almost seem good. We must stand our guard leaning on the Holy Spirit remembering when Jesus told his disciples,

> *Beware of false prophets, who come to you in sheep's clothing, but are ravenous wolves … .A good tree cannot bear bad fruit, nor can a rotten tree bear good fruit.*
>
> (Matthew 7:15-17)

In closing this chapter, I'd like to share some insights on discernment and spiritual growth, as shared by Cardinal Raniero Cantalamessa, Preacher of the Papal Household, to Pope Francis and members of the Roman Curia. After explaining how the Holy Spirit speaks to us as a whisper, he reminded all of St. Ignatius of Loyola, who taught:

What comes from the Spirit of God brings with it joy, peace, tranquility, sweetness, simplicity, light. What comes from the spirit of evil, instead brings with it disturbance, agitation, anxiety, confusion, darkness, but it is true that in practice things are more complex. Inspiration can come from God, and despite that, cause great disturbance. But this is not due to the inspiration, which is sweet and peaceful like everything that comes from God. Rather it is born from resistance to the inspiration or from the fact that we are not ready to do what we are asked to do. However, if inspiration is accepted, the heart will soon find itself in a deep peace. God rewards every little victory in this area by making the soul feel its approval, which is the most beautiful thing, the purest joy that exists in this world. [2]

Key Takeaways

- **Spiritual Maturity:** How "fleshy" am I? Am I an infant in Christ? Am I growing in Christ? Take time each week to reflect on your spiritual journey. Consider areas where you have grown in your faith and still struggle. Engage in regular prayer and Bible reading to deepen your relationship with Christ, asking the Holy Spirit for guidance in your growth.

- **The Role of Scripture and Church Teachings:** Can I see how Scripture and Church teachings help me grow spiritually and align my desires with God's desires for me? Set aside a daily or weekly time to read and reflect on Scripture, focusing on verses that speak to God's will for your life. Attend Mass regularly and participate in Church teachings, whether through Bible studies, spiritual talks, or catechesis. Take notes during homilies or teachings that speak to you, and reflect on how they align with God's plan for your life.

- **Cardinal Virtues in Discernment:** Do I consider the cardinal virtues in my life when discerning something? Why or why not? Spend time praying for God to help you practice these virtues daily, using them as a foundation for your discernment.

- **The Holy Spirit's Influence:** How do I see the Holy Spirit working in and through me in my daily life? Throughout the day, stay mindful of the Holy Spirit's presence by taking brief moments to pause and ask, "Holy Spirit, what are You guiding me to do in this moment?" Perhaps consider keeping a journal to track times you feel led by the Holy Spirit—whether in small decisions or significant moments of discernment.

References:
[1] St. John Chrysostom, *Ecloga de Oration* 2: 63,585

[2] Cindy Wooden, *Discernment is Essential to Discipleship, Papal Preacher Says*, CNS March 22, 2024

Chapter 3:

Recognizing God's Voice

Where to Begin

Recently my friend Jeff vented about the relentless noise that envelopes our lives. He shared, "The noise is constant. Work. School. Family. Breakfast. Lunch. Dinner. Sleep. Repeat. Between those we fill in with television, music, podcasts, video games, internet surfing, and scrolling. Always scrolling. And then there's drink or drugs." It struck me how accurately Jeff captured the chaotic rhythm of our daily existence. Jeff continued, "Or the 24-hour news cycle competing for our attention so that every event becomes a world-ending crisis. It's like mortar between the bricks in our day until we build a wall of noise that we let block God's voice."

I agree with my friend, and I think many of us feel or have felt the same. This world can be tiring, leading us to things and places we do not wish to go. As our anxieties grow, a feeling of uneasiness becomes ever-present, and fear can take hold. We long to cry out to God for guidance, yet we are often unsure how to approach Him.

So where to begin; where do you and I begin a new journey; a new journey where we are able to tune into God's guidance in this noisy world? Where and how do we start discerning what God is calling us to do? How do we begin to hear his voice?

I'm reminded of Nike's famous ad campaign: *Just Do It*. A three-word campaign that Nike executives insisted was not a slogan; but rather, it was their philosophy. Perhaps this philosophy, this mantra, could be applied to our spiritual lives as we open ourselves to new possibilities and decide to take our first or next step toward God.

The beautiful truth is that you don't have to wait for the perfect moment to take that next step towards God. In fact, you deciding to start makes it the perfect moment. So, start right here, right now, in the middle of your busy crazy messy life; your beautiful busy crazy messy life. This is the place, and this is the time that God has gifted you. Embrace it. This is your time. Know and focus on your purpose: to discover and align your deepest desires with His divine will; to uncover what I like to call your God Self heart, and what the Catholic Church calls, "our hidden center."

> *The heart is our hidden center…the place of decision, deeper than our psychic drive. It is the place of truth, where we choose life or death. It is the place of encounter, because as image of God we live in relation: it is the place of covenant.*
>
> (CCC, 2563).

Our Hidden Center

"Our Hidden Center" refers to the deepest essence of who we are as individuals in relation to one another and to our Creator. This hidden center, this true heart, created for each one of us by God defines us. It marks the part of us inherently linked to God, reflecting His love, goodness, and purpose. This heart is not merely an abstract concept; it is a vital aspect of our identity that shapes our thoughts, emotions, and actions. It is the place we encounter agape love…it is the place we encounter God.

And the heart is "the place of covenant," a place where relationships are formed and nurtured. The heart is the place where our loved ones live. Our heart, our hidden center, is the place where love abides. It is the place where we grow as children of God. As the Book of Genesis states, we are created in God's image and likeness (Genesis 1:27). This foundational truth suggests that within each of us lies a reflection of God's character. Our heart embodies qualities such as love, compassion, creativity, and the capacity for deep connection with others and God Himself.

Our hidden center is our internal compass, guiding us towards truth and righteousness. It is the source of our intuition and moral understanding, helping us discern right from wrong. We can become more attuned to God's will and guidance by cultivating a relationship with this divine aspect of ourselves. Recognizing and embracing our hidden center is an invitation to wholeness. It encourages us to integrate our spiritual, emotional, and physical selves, fostering a holistic approach to life. It is the only place where we can love God, allow Him to love us, and love our neighbor. When we nurture this connection, through prayer and reflection, we are then able to go about our days better hearing His voice and seeing His face in all who we share our community with.

Remind yourself daily of God's presence. While driving, while walking down the sidewalk, while sitting at your desk take a moment to acknowledge that He is with you. Look for the face of God in every encounter and you'll find Him. See the face of Jesus in the face of the Uber driver and the Starbucks' barista, in cooking mac and cheese for the kids, in the joyful eyes of your dog as you play fetch.

Whisper to God often and listen for His whispered reply. Open your heart and take in His beautiful creation that surrounds you. Cherish your open heart, that will help you keep it open, that will help you keep it aligned with His heart.

Make time and space for prayer. At prayer time, in your own sacred space, take a crucifix, light a candle, grab your bible or a book that inspires you. Invite the Holy Spirit into your sacred space - welcome Him, thank Him, love Him.

And recall what Jesus told us on how our prayers are answered,

> *And I tell you, ask and you will receive; seek and you will find; knock and the door will be opened to you. For everyone who asks, receives; and the one who seeks, finds; and the one who knocks, the door will be opened*
>
> (Luke 11:9-10)

When we "Just Do It," when we make a promise to ourselves to accept that this is our time, this is our place, and it is a gift from God, the holiness of everything in our lives begins to unveil. Our ordinary lives begin to grow, and it is right, and it is beautiful, and it is holy. This is what prayer does, this is what discernment is, this is living from our Hidden Center. The first thing we need to do is to just show up…Just Do It.

God and His Spirit often speak in whispers. True he speaks to us through others, but he does seem to like whispering, preferring the intimacy of our hearts. Just as Jesus showed us in his life, quiet alone time with God is essential in growing your relationship; it's essential in aligning our hearts with His.

Practical Steps to Quieting Ourselves

To help quiet our minds and prepare ourselves to listen to God's voice, consider these practical steps:

- **Create a Prayer Space at Home:** Designate a specific area for prayer and reflection. Include a comfortable chair, a side table with a Bible, a candle, maybe a rosary or other sacramental that creates a peaceful atmosphere.

- **Turn Off Your Phone:** In our hyper-connected world, it's crucial to disconnect from distractions. Turn off your phone instead of simply silencing it; this will help eliminate interruptions.

- **Invite the Holy Spirit In:** Make it a habit to invite the Holy Spirit into your prayer time. Ask for guidance, wisdom, and clarity in your life.

- **Practice Mindful Breathing:** Spend a few moments focusing on your breath. Breathe in slowly, paying attention to your body, heart, mind, and spirit. Invite the Holy Spirit in with your inhale and release your anxieties with your exhale.

Seeking God Beyond Your Home

Even when you're away from home, there are ways to seek God's presence:

- **Spend Time in Adoration:** Find a local chapel or church that offers adoration where you can spend time with Jesus, listening to Him and deepening your relationship with Him.

- **Take Nature Walks:** Spend time outdoors, appreciating the beauty of God's creation, and listen for His voice in the tranquility of nature.

- **Arrive Early or Stay Late at Mass:** Use this time to soak in the sacred atmosphere. Sit and take in the stained-glass windows, the baptismal font, the statues, the stations, the altar, the crucifix, and finally the tabernacle allowing the presence of Jesus to fill your heart.

- **Consider a Silent Retreat:** If you can, attend a silent retreat to deepen your relationship with God in solitude.

As We Walk with Him

God yearns to speak to each of us and walk with us. If we listen, we will hear his whisper. He will guide us to where we long to go. Through times of beauty and times of trial, even terror, He is there with us. Open your heart, let God work within you, just keep going and trust in Him.

When we take God's hand, when we walk with God, he will never lead us in the wrong direction; it's impossible for Him to do that. God created you in His image and likeness, He loves you more than you will ever know. He wants the very best for you; that is to say, He wants your heart and its deepest desires to align with His heart and deepest desires. This is God's will.

Key Takeaways

- **Reflect on Noise**: What noise and distractions keep you from hearing God's voice? Identify specific sources of distraction that may be preventing you from connecting with your hidden center.

- **Bring Anxieties to God**: What anxieties are you experiencing, and how might you bring those to God? Recognize that expressing your concerns is a way to align your heart with God's peace and clarity.

- **Embrace Your Hidden Center**: How can you cultivate awareness of your hidden center…your place of truth? Reflect on the divine qualities within you and consider how they guide your decisions and desires.

- **Make Time for Jesus**: How can you create more time for Jesus daily? Seek to incorporate moments of prayer, reflection, and connection that nurture your relationship with Him and your inner self.

- **Listen for the Holy Spirit**: How can you practice listening more attentively to the Holy Spirit's whispers? Create spaces of stillness in your life where you can hear God's guidance and deepen your understanding of your purpose.

Chapter 4:

The Role of Prayer in Discernment

> *My secret is very simple: I pray. Through prayer, I become one in love with Christ. I realize that praying to Him is loving Him.* St. Mother Teresa [1]

I'm on a retreat waiting in line for confession. It's now my turn, so I enter the confessional, sit down, and smiling at the priest, I say, "Hello, Father." He looks into my eyes and asked, "How are you, David?"

This priest I find myself in front of is also a dear friend of mine, someone I love and deeply respect. I begin my confession. After confessing my sins I say, "Father, there's this one last sin that I struggle with and it is this; there are times when I find it hard to pray, and what follows are thoughts in my mind asking, or rather believing, that I am not loving God with all my heart, soul, mind and strength. Because if I'm being 100% honest, sometimes I feel that way; that there are times when I don't love Him with all my heart, soul, mind, and strength." Gazing back into my eyes, this dear priest, this friend of mine lovingly replies, "Welcome to the club."

"Welcome to the club." Those words that night in the confessional have remained with me and always will. This priest I admired, who I thought of as a living saint, struggled with the same challenges.

We all struggle with it, don't we? Being faithful to our prayer time and to our relationship with God can, at times, seem difficult. But like any friendship, we must care for it, nurture it, participate in it, and be there for our friend, knowing that He is always there for us; that's true friendship. That's true love.

So, how do you and I develop a healthy and mature prayer life? How do we build a daily habit of prayer and make it the center of our lives and grow our relationship with God? To pray to God is to love God. If we can develop a healthy prayer life, a mature prayer life, then it will be in our prayer where we will confidently be able to discern what God indeed wants for us. We will know He is right here with us; guiding us to do what He made us to do, to fulfill His purpose for our lives.

About now, some of you may be thinking, "Ok Deacon, 'Just Do It,' as you mentioned in the last chapter sounds all good and well, it may even be motivating, and I may be ready to begin or to begin anew, but what else can you give me? Where do I begin? How do I stay the course?" What kind of prayer will work for me?

First, Let's Look to the Church

> *In one's prayer life, the Church in her wisdom, defines three major expressions of prayer: Vocal Prayer, Meditation, and Contemplative Prayer.*

> *"They have one basic trait in common: composure of heart. This vigilance in keeping the Word and dwelling in the presence of God makes these three expressions intense times in the life of prayer.*

> (CCC, 2699)

Vocal Prayer

When we pray vocally, we speak, which is something us humans like to do. Jesus taught us the most important vocal prayer, the Our Father. And there are many times in the gospels where Jesus prayed directly to His Father and should be our example.

The beauty of vocal prayer lies in the words we say and the intention behind them. It's helpful to remember it's not the length or eloquence of our prayers that matters to God but the sincerity with which we offer them. A simple prayer, spoken from the heart with love and devotion, might be more meaningful than a lengthy, impersonal one. As St. John Chrysostom wisely noted,

> *Whether or not our prayer is heard depends not on the number of words but on the fervor of our souls.*

> (CCC 2700).

Vocal prayers are not only for moments of deep need or emergency. They are a way to engage with God regularly, creating a rhythm of communication in our lives. Whether reciting formal prayers like the Our Father, praying for others, or simply speaking to God in the quiet of our hearts, vocal prayer allows us to maintain an ongoing connection with our Creator. This active participation in worship helps foster a deeper relationship with God, allowing us to grow in faith, trust, and understanding.

Prayer is a dialogue, we speak to our Lord and then we listen for His voice. Vocal prayer is me standing in front of my God saying, "Here I am, Lord," and then listening; listening for His voice in that time of silence and listening for His voice as I go about my day.

Meditation

Meditative prayer *is above all a quest*. We can use scripture, or liturgical books to help us in our meditation. As we faithfully practice our meditative prayer we discover,

> *... the movements that stir the heart and we are able to discern them. It is a question of acting truthfully in order to come into the light: 'Lord, what do you want me to do?'*

(CCC 2705 - 2706)

Of all meditative prayers, the Rosary is the most popular and powerful. As we gently pray the beads, we meditate on the key events in Christ's life, moving through the joyful, sorrowful, and glorious mysteries. Each mystery helps us reflect on different aspects of Christ's life and His love for us. As we focus on these events, we are invited to not only deepen our knowledge of Christ but also draw nearer to Him, allowing His life to intertwine with ours.

When we make the Rosary a regular part of our prayer life, we may witness transformation in our spiritual lives. Slowing down and reflecting on Christ's life in this way brings peace, insight, and clarity. Over time, we may notice our relationship with God growing, our discernment sharpening, and our hearts becoming more attuned to His desires. Meditative prayer, like the Rosary, is a beautiful way to journey with God and hear His voice more clearly in our daily lives. Pray the Rosary often and see your spiritual life grow.

Contemplative Prayer

Me being face to face, knee to knee with Jesus: that's contemplative prayer. It's spending time with my friend Jesus, whom I love. It's spending time with my Lord, who I have complete confidence in. Confidence like the child at the grocery store who when walking down the aisle with his father, stops to look at the candy while his father keeps going to the dairy section. Moments go by and the child realizing that his father is no longer with him begins to yell, "Daddy where are you…come back and pick me up daddy," knowing with complete confidence that his father will hear him and be right there to indeed pick him up. That's the kind of confidence we should have in our relationship with God; a confidence that he is always with us, and that's the kind of confidence we experience in contemplative prayer.

> *Contemplative is a gaze of faith, fixed on Jesus.*
>
> (CCC, 2715)

We fix our eyes on Jesus and experience his love as he gazes back into our hearts. In these silent times of prayer, Jesus' gaze begins to purify our hearts, and our love and desire to follow Jesus increases. We are able to stand before Jesus, and confidently answer, "Yes!" to Jesus' "follow me."

In all three forms of prayer—vocal, meditative, and contemplative—we invite the Holy Spirit in, we listen to Him, we hear Him, we align our deepest desires with His.

> *By prayer we can discern 'what is the will of God' and obtain the endurance to do it. Jesus teaches us that one enters the kingdom of heaven not by speaking words, but by doing 'the will of my Father in heaven.'*
>
> (CCC 2826)

As we practice these forms of prayer, we allow the Holy Spirit to guide us, helping us align our will with God's and strengthening us to follow His plan for our lives. Through these spiritual practices, we come to know God's will more clearly and gain the courage to live it out.

Next, Let's Look to the Journey...Your Journey

The road to discernment is led by, driven by, and consumed by prayer. Just as the Church has its seasons, so to do our prayer lives...or our prayer journey.

The Church year consists of six liturgical seasons: Advent, Christmas, Ordinary Time after the Epiphany, Lent, Easter, and finally back to Ordinary Time after Pentecost.

The Church's seasons begin with Advent; a time of excitement as we wait and prepare for the coming of Jesus; we look to the beauty of the Incarnation and to His second and final coming. Next, Christmas; a time of rejoicing in the birth of our Savior. Following Jesus's baptism is Ordinary Time where we focus on his early life and childhood and on to His public ministry. On Ash Wednesday through Holy Saturday we turn to Lent, the penitential season of the Church which recalls the 40 days Jesus spent in the desert and the forty years the Israelites wandered in the desert. Lent brings us through the events leading up to Christ's Passion and to the Passion itself. Finally, we celebrate the joyous season of Easter where we celebrate Christ's resurrection, ascension to heaven and Pentecost. Lastly, we move to the second period of Ordinary Time where we recognize Christ as the King of kings and the age of the Church. Beginning with the age of the Apostles this is the age we are still living in today for which we are ever preparing for His second coming.

Our prayer journey also consists of seasons. Seasons of ordinary moments as we walk side-by-side with Jesus in our everyday lives, our ordinary lives, getting to know Him more and more and learning what He desires of us. But it's not always ordinary, if we continue the journey, we will discover and experience other seasons: seasons and times of preparation, beauty, even incarnation. Yes, there will be seasons of agony and penance. But continue the journey, keep your hand held in His, for there too will come beautiful seasons of forgiveness, mercy, and yes - resurrection.

Will you say yes to being that beloved child of God that he has made you to be? Will you begin or renew the commitment, your personal "Just Do It," of making prayer a daily importance in your life? This is your choice, and in choosing to say yes, you are saying yes God I desire to live out all the seasons of my life; I choose to live a life of discernment.

Starting the Journey: Conversations with God

I come home in the evening, greet my wife with a kiss, and ask about her day. We share how our days went, what we did, what we didn't get a chance to do. Maybe we talk about someone we met that day, maybe someone we were able to help or who was able to help us. Our conversation might shift to our kids, parents or weekend plans. Occasionally we talk about a vacation or something happening at the parish. Some days our conversations may be fun and lighthearted; others may be on the more serious side. Sometimes, she may ask for my help; other times I may ask for hers.

There are some days when I may already know what I want to talk about when I get home, but on many days, I have no idea. Regardless, we have this routine; we visit everyday, whether cooking dinner or just winding down. We talk, and that conversation can lead to anywhere. The point is we are a committed married couple who love one another, and every day we start and participate in conversations. We enjoy visiting, we enjoy each other's company, and we grow with each other, little by little every day.

The same dynamic should hold true in our relationship with God. Prayer is conversation like the ones I share with my wife. You don't need to have it all figured out; just start the conversation with God…Just do it. Once the conversation starts, only God knows where it will end, and that's the beauty of it; God will lead that conversation to where it is supposed to go. God will lead you to where you are supposed to go.

Be his friend, start the conversation, and be awed at the life He has in store for you.

Less Me, More You, Lord

For many of us, as we begin our prayer time, we typically turn to God and ask Him for things we think we need or want, some serious things, and some not-so serious things, maybe even silly things. We may pray for our brother and ask God to help him with his addiction one night; that's rather serious. The next day we may be at our son's baseball game and pray that his team wins; not so serious. We may be running errands and pray for the unknown person who passes by us in an ambulance asking God to be with that person, and then we may pull into the grocery store parking lot and ask God to help us find a good parking space. That person in the ambulance may really need our prayers; you and I getting a good parking space – God's got better things to attend to.

With the many pressing issues of our world—wars, violence, climate change, and the suffering of countless people—it's essential to reflect on the nature of our petitions. Are we praying in a way that reflects the gravity of what's happening in the world? Are we thinking deeply about the needs of others or focusing on minor concerns that, while real, might not carry the same weight as more significant issues?

As our prayer life continues to grow, and we begin in prayer to reflect on our days, it is here that our prayer time begins to prosper as giving thanks and asking for God's mercy become more important to us. We may now begin our prayer in thanksgiving, thanking God for all he has done for us and all he has given us. Next, we hopefully turn to asking for forgiveness that we need and praying for His mercy. Then we probably move on to our petitions. Next, maybe we end with the Our Father and an Amen. Our prayer life, our relationship with God is growing.

If we continue to pray, continue our conversation with God, there will come a point where we will experience a change; you could call it a spiritual paradigm shift; a life changing moment in our relationship with Him, and this shift is when we stop asking God for what we want and begin asking Him what He wants. It is at this point that our desires become his desires. It is at this point that we come closer in discerning what He wants us to do, and we may begin to hear just what it is that He is saying to us.

We may move from asking, "God, please help my brother with his addiction," to, "God what do you want me to do to help my brother?" From, "God please help me and my wife in our troubled marriage, to, "God what do you think I should do to grow and better my relationship with my wife?"

This doesn't mean that we never ask God for anything, and it doesn't at all mean that we cease thanking God for his many blessings. And of course, we continue to ask for his forgiveness and mercy in our conversations, but things now seem different. And as we continue down this path, we more and more find ourselves asking God for his advice and we fear less-and-less on allowing him to guide us. Being finally able to sit face to face with him, finally able to gaze lovingly at him and receiving his loving gaze in return, finally able to allow his desires to be our desires, we find ourselves not so concerned about our wants and desires as our concerns have now turned to what He wants. It is here where we reach this spiritual paradigm shift, where we no longer fear asking Him, "God, what do you want me to do with my life?"

> *... yet not as I will, but as You will"*
>
> (Matthew 26:39)

Key Takeaways

- **How might I show more love for God in my prayer life?** How might I better prioritize my daily conversations with God? Can I find just a few moments each day to intentionally connect with Him through prayer?

- **What type of prayer works best for me, and why?** Experiment with different forms of worship—vocal, meditative, and contemplative. See which resonates with your heart. For example, try vocal prayers like the Our Father and other catholic prayers, engage in meditative prayer using Scripture or the Rosary, or spend quiet time in contemplative prayer, time with Jesus. Observe which style helps you feel closer to God and more attuned to His will.

- **Do I find it easier to talk to God or to listen to Him?** Reflect on your prayer habits—do you focus more on speaking or listening? If you tend to talk more, practice giving God the space to speak to your heart. Try sitting silently for a few minutes during your prayer time, allowing His presence to fill the space.

- **What might my life look like if I could ask, "God, what do You want me to do with my life?"** Reflect on the impact of surrendering your desires and asking

God what He wants you to do. Set aside time for deep prayer and reflection on your vocation, relationships, and purpose. Let this question guide your decisions in both big and minor aspects of life.

References:
[1] Mother Teresa, *Do Something Beautiful For God, The Essential Teachings of Mother Teresa*, Blue Sparrow Publishing 2020, p. 40

Chapter 5:

Discernment in Daily Life

How Present am I in His Presence?

As we continue to grow in our daily prayer life, we grow in love, God grows in us, and we begin to sense his presence in ordinary moments throughout our day. As we make prayer a consistent part of our daily routine, we begin to realize God's presence in ways we previously may not have. How present am I in His presence? That's an important question to routinely ponder. Ponder it often and notice God's presence throughout your day:

I felt God's presence this morning as I drank my coffee and looking out into my yard saw the red flames of a cardinal against the green leaves of an oak tree.

I felt God's presence this afternoon while shopping at the supermarket when a child looked at me and smiled.

I felt God's presence this evening as I looked down at my dog's face, into her eyes, and she gazed back into my eyes.

We come to realize that prayer is not just something we commit to every morning and evening, rather prayer becomes a way of life. To be a prayerful discerning disciple is to live in the presence of God. The more we commit ourselves to daily prayer time, the more we recognize that He walks with us. And as we recognize He is with us throughout the day, as we draw closer and closer to God, we are better able to discern His will, and we begin to realize the true beauty of life.

Draw near to God and he will draw near to you.

(James 4:8)

Here's how you can start noticing God's presence in your everyday moments:

- **Start with a Simple Prayer:**
  Begin each day by inviting God into your heart and your day. A simple prayer like, "God, I open myself to Your presence today. Please guide me and help me see You in everything I do" can help set the tone for the day and make you more aware of His presence.

- **Be Mindful of the Little Moments:**
  As you go through your day, pause, and notice the little blessings around you. A quiet moment with a friend, a slow walk in nature, or even a challenging situation can be an opportunity to sense God's presence and listen for His guidance.

- **Engage in Conversations with God:**
  View your daily conversations and activities as opportunities for prayer. When interacting with others, ask God for the grace to speak and listen with love. Whether it's a work meeting, a family dinner, or an interaction with a stranger, see it

as a chance to connect with God.

- **Reflect and Give Thanks:** At the end of the day, take a moment to reflect on how you saw God in your day. What moments stood out to you? What small acts of kindness or beauty did you experience? Offer your thanks for the ways He showed up in your life.

- **Cultivate a Listening Heart:** Prayer isn't just about talking to God; it's also about listening. Spend moments throughout your day in quietness, simply listening for God's voice. You might hear Him through Scripture, through a feeling of peace, or the words of others.

My phone buzzed with a text from my friend Ray: "Loving God today I offer my work for my friend David. May the work I do today be done with love for You and my friend David as he struggles with…" WOW! Talk about a prayer! How much comfort did my friend Ray bring me in sending me that text; in offering his workday for me! How pleasing was Ray and his prayer to God! This is what St. Paul means by,

Pray without ceasing.

(1 Thessalonians 5:17)

Everything can be and should be prayer because we are always in His presence as Jesus promised,

I am with you always, until the end of the age.

(Matthew 28:20)

Everything Can Be Prayer

Everything can be prayer. Bathing the dog, writing a term paper, picking up the kids from school, going on a date with your wife, helping your child with her homework, leading a sales presentation; everything can be prayer. Offering intentions as we go about our day in all we do: for loved ones, for our church, for our clergy, for the problems our nation faces, for those affected by a natural disaster, for the sick, for the imprisoned, for our enemies…the list is endless. This is how we continue to recognize His presence. This is how we continue the beautiful spiritual journey that God has gifted us. This is how our prayer life becomes our way of life. And most importantly, this is what leads us to truly being able to hear just what it is that God is calling us to do.

How Present am I in Other's Presence?

For where two or three are gathered together in my name, there am I in the midst of them.

(Matthew 18:20)

Jesus is present when we gather together, and He likes to speak to us through others. This is a beautiful invitation to recognize that Jesus is here and present in our relationships, whether with family, friends, or strangers.

Every morning, part of my prayer goes something like this, "Jesus help me to be your light to everyone I cross paths with today, to everyone I work with today, and please help me to see your light in them." In my life, I do want to be present for others. I'm not always good at it, but I know that I need to avail myself to others recognizing Jesus' presence is with us.

Yes, our God does indeed like to whisper to us, but our God is a communal God. God created us to smile at one another, to hold hands with one another, to hug one another, to hold one another. He created us to laugh with one another, to cry with one another, to celebrate with one another and to grieve with one another. We were created to be together, not alone. As the Church teaches us, *"On coming into the world, man is not equipped with everything he needs for developing his bodily and spiritual life. He needs others."*

(CCC, 1936). From the beginning, God recognized that, *"It is not good for the man to be alone,"* (Genesis 2:18) so he created Eve, a companion for Adam.

God made us this way. You and I are part of the Body of Christ. We are living inside this incarnation and just as we need God, we need one another. We need people. People we can see and touch and look into their eyes and relate to; even people we may disagree with. Why? Because God often speaks to us through others and uses us to speak to others for Him.

God created us, giving us hearts and souls that long for Him, and it is in that longing that we pray and discern His will. And after our prayer, after we understand what God wants us to do, we are then sent - sent out to our families, workplaces, communities, and beyond. Through us, He speaks to others, and they, in turn, will speak to us. We become His hands and feet, fulfilling His mission in our world. This is our communal God. This is our Trinitarian God.

A More Peaceful and Fulfilled Life

God wants you to live an abundant life, a peaceful fulfilling life. In living a life following Jesus and discerning what God wants you to do with your life; you will find fulfillment; you will find peace. Will there be challenges? Yes. Will there be times of despair, distress, even agony?

Yes. Will there be valleys on the journey where you may be wounded along the way? Yes. But remember our Savior agonized in the garden and was nailed to, suffered and died on a cross…for our sake.

In discerning and following God's will we remain people of hope. We remain people of the resurrection. We remain Easter people. And just as Jesus' wounds from the cross were healed, so too will He heal our wounds. God is love, and as St. Paul taught us,

> *Love is patient, love is kind…it rejoices with the truth. It bears all things, believes all things, hopes all things, endures all things.*

(1 Corinthians 13:4,6)

In discerning God's will, we discern His love, and as we go out to do His will, we will find love, we will experience love, and we will share His love. We will find peace in Him and in one another. We will live lives of abundance with days full of both receiving His love and sharing His love. We will live fulfilling lives.

Key Takeaways

- **Am I committed to morning and evening prayer?** Reflect on your current commitment to prayer. Consider setting aside intentional time each morning and evening, even just a few minutes. Start by finding a quiet space and making prayer a non-negotiable part of your daily routine. If you find it hard to start, try setting a reminder on your phone or journal about your prayer intentions to hold yourself accountable.

- **Where am I in my prayer becoming my way of life?** Evaluate whether prayer is a regular part of your life or something you do occasionally. Ask yourself, "How can I make prayer more consistent and a natural part of my routine?" You might start by weaving prayer into everyday tasks—praying while commuting, doing chores, or before meals. You could also consider setting a regular time for prayer, such as midday or just before bedtime, to keep it a consistent part of your day.

- **How often do I feel God's presence as I go about my day?** Start noticing the small, everyday moments where God's presence might be felt. Practice mindfulness by pausing during your day to reflect on God's presence.

- **How present am I to my family and others?** Are there times when I am physically there but mentally elsewhere? How might I make more of a conscious effort to give my full attention to my family, my friends and those I work with? How often do I recognize God's presence in others?

Chapter 6:

Obstacles to Discernment

Shaking my hand as he was leaving the church after mass, Bill said to me, "I admit I sometimes find myself among the thorns, but oh how I do desire to find rich soil," I replied, "I know, we all do."

We had just read the Parable of the Sower from the Gospel of Luke, Jesus explained:

> *This is the meaning of the parable. The seed is the word of God. Those on the path are the ones who have heard, but the devil comes and takes away the word from their hearts that they may not believe and be saved. Those on rocky ground are the ones who, when they hear, receive the word with joy, but they have no root; they believe only for a time and fall away in time of trial. As for the seed that fell among thorns, they are the ones who have heard, but as they go along, they are choked by the anxieties and riches and pleasures of life, and they fail to produce mature fruit. But as for the seed that fell on rich soil, they are the ones who, when they have heard the word, embrace it with a generous and good heart, and bear fruit through perseverance.*
>
> (Luke 8:11-15)

Obstacles will inevitably arise on our spiritual journeys. We will encounter challenges along the way. They may be fear or impatience, doubt or anxiety, and sometimes just plain tiredness. They will appear, sometimes unexpectedly, and we may find ourselves asking, "Why do I sometimes find myself on this path that I know I should not be on? How do I get off this rocky ground? How do I get through these thorns and get back to the rich soil?"

We all want to be part of the rich soil. Our desire is to be good and holy. When we open our hearts, we provide a rich place for the seeds, the Word of the Sower, to take root and flourish. When we are on rich soil our prayer life, our discernment is where it needs to be; we are growing and are at peace. Realistically that is not always the case. Ask anyone who has attended an ACTS retreat, or any other meaningful retreat or spiritual high, and has come back on fire. The initial excitement does wear off and signs of dryness and bareness may show up, and this likewise can occur many times on our discernment journey.

Looking back at the Parable of the Sower, our reaction may first turn to our own egos bringing thoughts of I need to get back to it, I need to improve my life, I need to love more, I need to pray more, I need to…, I need to…, I need to…STOP! This parable is not entitled, <u>The Parable of the Path, Ground, Thorn Bushes, and Soil</u>. It is entitled, <u>The Parable of the Sower</u>. Its focus is not on you and me; its focus is on the Sower. It is about God's abundant and constant generosity and kindness. This loving Sower seems to spread just as many seeds to the rich soil as he does to the rocks and the thorns. He doesn't seem to mind the condition of the pasture and the farm; his intent is to spread his Word everywhere and to everyone, no matter where one might currently find oneself.

Knowing that God is always with us spreading his Word; that's what we should always recall, especially when we find ourselves experiencing things that are hindering our prayer life; that are hindering our discernment.

Return to prayer, strive to be faithful to your prayer time knowing that He is there. God is with us, no matter where we might be. He always shows up, and so should we. Some days prayer will be easy and some days it will seem like a chore. Your discernment journey will be one of smooth trails and scree trails, uphill climbs and downhill rides, seemingly endless marathons and short easy sprints, long dry valleys and beautiful coastal sunrises. There will be times when the rain and wind pelt your face as you drive forward and times when you reach the peak of the mountain with the sun at your back. Just keep going.

Our spiritual journeys are journeys of peaks and valleys. Sometimes it will feel like one step forward and two steps back but stay the course. Will we revert back to just asking Him for things, neglecting to ask what he wants from us? Yes, we will. But stay faithful to your prayer time. These ups and downs, they are all part of the journey. Continue to embrace your prayer time, your discernment journey, and remember the last two words in Jesus's explanation of the Sower,

> *embrace it* (the Word) *with a generous and good heart, and bear fruit **through perseverance.***
> (Luke 8:15)

How to Persevere

Ronald Rolheiser, a Roman Catholic priest with the Missionary Oblates of Mary, and an international speaker and best-selling author has written extensively on prayer, and I share with you two of his thoughts on fidelity to prayer; writings that I have found particularly helpful.

In his book, *Prayer: Our Deepest Longing,* Fr. Ron compares prayer to falling in love. In the beginning it is easy, because *"love is sweet only in its initial stage,"* but as we grow in our relationship, *"reality begins to dispel an illusion."* He goes on to write, *"It's not that we become disillusioned with God, but rather we come to realize that so many of the warm thoughts and feelings we believed were about God were really about ourselves."* Fr. Ron says this disillusionment is good because it dispels our illusion. He goes on to say when this disillusionment occurs it is an actual maturing moment in our prayer lives. *"The easy response is to back away,"* because the whole thing has been an illusion. It is here when we start to find it hard to pray, when we may stop praying. But the opposite of discontinuing our prayer is the answer, and here is where we make a commitment to continue showing up. Like in any committed relationship:

> *"The deeper we go in relationships and prayer, the more unsure of ourselves we become, and this is the beginning of maturity. It's when I say, 'I don't know how to love,' and, 'I don't know how to pray,' that I first begin to understand what love and prayer actually are."* [1]

In his article entitled, *Some Advice on Prayer from an Old Master*, Fr. Ron speaks of advice he received from a professor he once had. There are days when we are tired, exhausted, involved with too many things, and it is hard to find the time and energy to quiet ourselves and just be with God. And on those difficult days, and at the risk of sounding too simplistic, try to pray one sincere Our Father; furthermore, try to sincerely pray at least one sincere Our Father each and every day in your prayer time. This prayer that Jesus gave us is a petition for others, and we are asked to pray daily for others.

Fr. Ron reminds us that none of us are divine. He closes writing, *"We're incurably human,"* filled with all kinds of distractions.

> *"Our prayer seldom issues forth from a pure heart but normally from a very earthy one. But, and this is the point, its very earthiness is also its real honesty. Our restlessness, distracted heart is also our existential heart and is the existential heart of the world. When we pray from there, we are lifting mind and heart to God."* [2]

Show up always, pray what you can, know that He is there, and on those really tough days, stay committed by being faithful to a moment of silence and praying an Our Father as best you can.

What if I'm Angry at God

There are events that occur in our lives, sad events, events we do not understand. We may find ourselves asking, maybe even screaming, "Why? Why God did you let this happen? We may find ourselves asking, "How can I pray to God when I am angry at Him; when I am hurt and mad at something I think He allowed to happen?" Some of us have been here and it is a tough place to be, an almost unbearable place to be.

Months after her daughter's funeral I found myself in front of Mary. "Is it ok to be angry with God? Why did God not answer my prayers? I prayed and prayed for my daughter to be ok…I don't understand why He did not answer my prayers?" she asked.

We shared a moment of silence.

I then responded, "I don't know."

Another moment of silence.

"But here is what I do know. I know God hears every single prayer. All of them. From everyone. I know God loves us all and hates our suffering probably more than we do, like you do with your daughter Sophia. And I know people who have prayed for healing, provision, answers, and more, and gotten none of the specific things they have asked for. I know others who have experienced miraculous healing and provision and wonders, but I don't know why. And I also know that it is ok to be angry with God. Telling God you are mad at him is not sinful and it might be the most honest form of prayer; it takes great trust and patience because it is honesty at its rawest."

Taking her hands and looking into her tearing eyes, I continued, "What I also know is that in answer to every prayer, God sends his Spirit, which Jesus called your Advocate who will be with you always. Mary, use the gift of faith that you have been given. Trust, surrender, and just sit with God for a while. In your sadness and in your anger, especially in your anger, sit with him, and I think you'll find a satisfying answer. It's not giving up. It's not losing. It can feel like it; it can feel like letting go, but as you move to and accept God's grace that question may be answered...and that anger may soften. Keep praying Mary."

In the toughest times of our lives, when we may find ourselves screaming at God, "Why!" When we may find ourselves not giving an ounce of care to what He wants; keep screaming, keep yelling, keep asking, keep turning to Him…His grace will follow.

Key Takeaways

- **Reflect on Luke 8:4-15 -** Take out your bible and read Luke 8: 4-15. Invite the Holy Spirit in. Read the passage again.
    - What thoughts come to mind when reading and reflecting on this scripture?
    - What might God want you to take from this scripture passage?

- **Identify Your Current Spiritual State:** Reflect on where you are in your faith journey right now. What path do you currently find yourself on?
    - Are there areas where you truly feel blessed and close to God?
    - Are there any areas where you may feel spiritually dry or distracted?
    - What steps can you take to open your heart where God's Word might take root and grow?

- **Perseverance in Discernment:** Reflect on your personal perseverance in discernment
    - Are there any challenges you may be facing?
    - How might you go about addressing those challenges?

- **Bringing Your Anger to God:** If you've ever been angry at God, take some time to reflect on that experience.

- How did you process your feelings of anger or frustration?
- How did you overcome that anger and find peace?

References:
[1] Ronald Rolheiser, *Prayer: Our Deepest Longing* (Franciscan Media, 2013), pp. 44-46
[2] Ronald Rolheiser, *Some Advice on Prayer from an Old Master*, www.ronrolheiser.com, May 31, 2020

Chapter 7:

Spiritual Formation and Its Role in Discernment

As you and I form spiritually, we are drawn into a closer and deeper relationship with God, and in doing so we will gain a greater discernment of God's desire for our lives. It is through prayer, scripture reading and reflection, spiritual direction, participation in the sacraments, and finally action, the way we live our lives, that we spiritually mature. A well-practiced spiritual life takes time and devotion, but if we trust in the Holy Spirit to guide us, our lives will blossom into a well-formed spiritual life, and if we continue to rely on the Holy Spirit, and continue to listen to Jesus, He will lead us on this journey to becoming a spiritually mature person. This spiritual maturity, and the road to it, doesn't just impact our relationship with God—it lovingly enhances every part of our lives: relationships with spouses, family and friends, our work, service to our church and community; every aspect of our lives is affected as we are molded into channels of Jesus' peace.

The Apostles' Spiritual Formation

In the Gospels and in Acts of the Apostles, we learn of the apostles' spiritual journeys, their discernment and how they came to be spiritually mature in their lives.

> *While he was still speaking, behold, a bright cloud cast a shadow over them, then from the cloud came a voice that said, "This is my beloved Son, with whom I am well pleased; listen to him." When the disciples heard this, they fell prostrate and were very much afraid. But Jesus came and touched them, saying, "Rise, and do not be afraid." And*

when the disciples raised their eyes, they saw no one else but Jesus alone.

(Matthew 17:5-8)

Peter, James and John first responded to the Transfigured Christ with fear. You and I, we're not much different. In the world we live in today; the climate crisis, gun violence, wars, hateful politics; this is where many of us are today, living in a world of fear. For the disciples, living in an occupied territory, and everything that entailed, they too lived in a world of fear; that's where their journey with Jesus began, that's where their spiritual journey began. Living in this occupied territory, and then meeting Jesus, following Jesus and all they experienced; their world had been turned upside down. It's no wonder their first reaction to Jesus's transformation and God's voice was fear.

"They fell prostrate and were very much afraid." But Jesus comes to them, touches them, and says, *"Rise and do not be afraid."* (Matthew 17:6-7) The three men rise, they look up, and all they see is this man they are falling in love with, Jesus. This is the Christ, gazing back at them, loving them, saying to them, "you are mine."

And what happens next? Jesus leads them back down the mountain to carry on and do his work, to do what he wants and needs them to do. Descending from the mountain, that sacred ground, having experienced this glorious sight of Jesus with Moses and Elijah, these three apostles likely now knew they were absolutely on a sacred journey. How much spiritual growth did these three experience that day? How much deeper did their relationship with Jesus grow that day? Where were they now in their spiritual formation? And most importantly, how attentively did they hear God's final three words, *"...listen to Him."* (Matthew 17:5)

Jesus led these three men on a sacred journey; from the sea of Galilee through his ministry to that mountain and then back down the mountain and beyond to fulfillment of what they were to do and who they were to become: men of virtue, men of humility, men of truth. Those three apostles, along with the other apostles continued their spiritual formation for the remainder of their lives.

Our Spiritual Formation

You and I, we too must journey to our own mountain top. It may take some difficult climbing, but if we persevere, we will reach it. We will experience our own transfiguration. We will feel God's presence. We will listen to God. Our spiritual life will grow and mature, and we too will be sent down the mountain to go and do God's work.

We grow in our spiritual maturity in discernment. This spiritual formation is a sacred journey, and it is sacred because we are not just flesh and blood. We are also spiritual beings. What other journey is there that a spirit could take other than a spiritual journey?

Spiritual maturity is not merely theology or knowledge of God, and it certainly is not simply good feelings towards God. St. Peter tells us:

> *For this very reason, make every effort to supplement your faith with virtue, virtue with knowledge, knowledge with self-control, self-control with endurance, endurance with devotion, devotion with mutual affection, mutual affection with love. If these are yours and increase in abundance, they will keep you from being idle or unfruitful in the knowledge of our Lord Jesus Christ.*

(2 Peter 1:5-8)

A spiritual mature person is one growing in virtue and humility. A spiritual mature person knows that they desire what God desires, and that their work is in praise and thanks to God. They truly give God all the glory while understanding and accepting that although they are striving to grow in perfection as He desires, their formation will continue and they will never fully reach complete maturity while on this earth, but they will continue to press on striving to grow in His eyes and for the benefit of His beloved children.

Spiritually mature Catholics do not miss mass, they observe holy days of obligation, teach their children and grandchildren the faith, go to confession when necessary, are committed to their prayer time and in growing closer to

God, and they live out their faith in their communities. A Catholic who strives to be committed to all of these knows that in their commitment they are building a deeper connection to discerning God's will. At the end of holy mass, when the deacon proclaims, "Go in Peace," a spiritually mature Catholic understands just what that means, and they then go out and do it.

Key Takeaways

- **Where am I in my spiritual formation?** Take time to reflect on your spiritual journey. Are you growing in your relationship with God, or do you feel stuck? If you feel stagnant, reflect on why you might feel that way and how might you bring those feelings to prayer

- **Do I desire a stronger connection to God's will?** Ask yourself if you are genuinely open to hearing what God desires for your life. If there is confusion, how might you bring that confusion to prayer?

- **What thoughts come to mind when I hear, "Your life is a spiritual journey?"** Reflect on how you perceive your life's spiritual path. Do you see it as a growth journey with ups and downs? Consider the changes you might want to make to better open your heart to God's transformative work.

- **What actions could I take to help me grow in my Catholic faith?** Think about the practical steps you can take to nurture your faith.

Chapter 8:

Cultivating a Discerning Heart

Nurturing Discernment

In Chapter 3, I discussed the importance of quieting ourselves to hear God's voice. I shared practical suggestions such as creating a prayer space, inviting the Holy Spirit in, and breathing in prayer. Now let's dive a little deeper into how to develop spiritual practices that nurture spiritual discernment and help us grow closer to God.

A commitment to daily solitude prayer is essential in cultivating and fostering one's spiritual discernment. The "Just do It" part does need a sincere initial commitment with a true and ongoing devotion to one's prayer time. Quiet morning and evening prayer, even midday prayer, where we talk with God, we practice meditative prayer, and we move closer to exercising and experiencing contemplative prayer are essential in hearing God's voice and in discerning His will.

Solitude in prayer doesn't mean being alone—it means being fully present to God, away from the distractions of daily life. Over time, this practice can deepen your relationship with Him, fostering spiritual growth, peace, and clarity. As you consistently show up for God, you'll hear His guidance more clearly and discern His will more deeply. Let these quiet moments of solitude become the foundation of your spiritual journey as you grow in the knowledge and love of God.

Begin small but make the commitment; ten minutes in the morning and ten minutes in the evening. If you are starting from zero minutes, spending ten minutes in the morning and ten in the evening is spending twenty times more time in minutes with God than before you started! Imagine what spiritual gifts might take root in just spending those few minutes with God. Commit to those minutes and see them grow; see your spiritual life grow. Those ten minutes will increase if you allow them. And how do you allow those ten minutes to increase and grow your relationship with God? You stay devoted to your prayer time, and you ask Him for His guidance and help.

Remain consistent and recognize any obstacles that may seem to hinder you in your solitude prayer time. Bring those supposed obstacles to prayer and ask God what you should do about these seemingly hurdles that you are encountering. Most importantly, be patient and try to refrain from becoming discouraged when you stumble, because you will stumble, and when you do, bring it to God and ask for help in starting afresh.

Reflecting on my prayer life and discernment journey, some of the best advice I received came from conversations with trusted friends, confessions with priests, and conversations with a deacon I knew well. However, the most profound guidance often came during my visits with my spiritual director. Seeking counsel from others—whether trusted mentors, priests, deacons, or spiritual directors—can be incredibly valuable. God often speaks to us through the wisdom and experience of others. Don't hesitate to reach out and seek guidance; you may be surprised by the insights and clarity that come through these conversations. Let these trusted voices help guide you as you discern God's will in your life.

Silence, Meditation, and Reflection

It's mid December 2012 and I had just returned from my first ACTS retreat. I was still buzzing from the experience, feeling the Holy Spirit like never before. But as the excitement began to settle, I asked, "Now what? Where do I go from here?"

A few days later I stumbled across a quote from St. John Paul II that stopped me: *"The biggest problem for Americans is that they do not know how to just be."* I felt certain that this quote wasn't just a coincidence; God had placed it before me for a reason. Later that evening, as I reflected on the quote, the thought of going to Adoration popped into my mind.

"Adoration? OK I'll go to adoration." So, a few days after Christmas, I found myself in front of the Blessed Sacrament. Somewhat uncomfortable and not knowing what to do or say I prayed the rosary, and then just sat there with the same recurring thoughts, questions, problems and desires residing in my head as they always had, and what did God say?...Nothing.

I went to adoration again , prayed more, prayed the same prayers I always had with the same thoughts, questions, problems and desires continuing to dwell in my head, still; nothing - AAAGGGHHH!

But I continued to go to adoration and just sit; just sit and be with Jesus – just "be".

Winter had turned to spring and during these past few months I had become involved with a couple of different ministries in my parish, I was making new friends, and I continued my prayer life and continued to go to adoration. During this time, I began to experience snippets of the Holy Spirit's presence in my days which brought bits of peace and beauty to my life, morsels of peace and beauty that I'm not sure I had ever experienced before – I longed for more.

Sitting in adoration one spring evening and thanking God for the new friends he had gifted me, it happened. God said, and this is where I know God has a sense of humor, because what God told me is something I often tell my boys. It's a phrase I'm known for, one my family teases me about for how often I say it. And when I say it to my boys, the response, always accompanied with rolling of eyes, goes something like, "I know dad…you always say that dad."

And just what was it that I finally heard God say…

"You're not paying attention, David."

"You're not paying attention. You need to pay attention to your heart." He continued, "I know you're trying, but when we visit you talk too much and don't listen enough. You need to listen to Me…listen to Me with your heart wide open."

That was a game-changer for me. I realized that silence is the key to listening. If we don't create space for stillness, we can't hear God. I had been so focused on speaking, praying, and asking for things that I wasn't giving God room to speak. Only when we quiet ourselves—when we stop talking long enough to listen—can we truly begin to hear His voice.

Be still and know that I am God!

(Psalm 46:11)

First, I sit in silence. Next, I learn to listen. Finally, I experience God's voice—I hear God

As we continue to listen to God, we grow in relationship, we grow in the understanding that we are made in His image and likeness, and it is then that we begin to see others in His love. This is discernment. This holy process, a personal spiritual journey each of us has been invited to experience by our Maker, each with its own path and timing as unique as each of us. And as we continue to listen to Him, He will continue to grow in us and we in Him. We will hear Him. We will know what it is that He wants us to do. And we will go out and do it.

Growing in Wisdom

As we grow in our prayer life turning away from the world for answers and turning to God for guidance and answers, our Triune God begins to share His wisdom with us. As we approach God in our discernment, we recall what Jesus said in Matthew,

> *Everyone who listens to these words of mine and acts on them will be like a wise man who built his house on rock.*
>
> (Matthew 7:24)

How comforting are Jesus's words that when we turn to Him, when we listen to Him and act on His words, He will share His wisdom with us. And as we grow closer to Jesus, continuing to listen and do what He asks us to do, the more wisdom He will share.

In the New Testament St. Paul and St. James amplify Jesus's teaching on wisdom. St. Paul, emphasizing our spirituality, invites us to listen and learn from the Holy Spirit. He writes,

> *We have not received the spirit of the world but the Spirit that is from God, so that we may understand the things freely given us by God. And we speak*

> *about them not with words taught by human
> wisdom, but with words taught by the Spirit,
> describing spiritual realities in spiritual terms.*
>
> (1 Corinthians 2: 12-13)

St. James, understanding that we will face times of trials and temptations, times when our foundations might begin to crack reminds us,

> *But if any of you lacks wisdom, he should ask God
> who gives to all generously and ungrudgingly, and
> he will be given it.*
>
> (James 1:5)

Knowing that God is eager to give us wisdom when we ask is reassuring. He doesn't withhold it or make us prove our worthiness. Instead, He gives generously, ready to help us navigate life with His insight.

Will the wisdom we ask for and the wisdom we gain always be easy to live out? No. Will there be times when we know what we should do but choose to do otherwise? Probably. And in these times, we will remember to come back to our merciful God; our God whose desire is for us to live lives of wisdom: peaceful, happy and fruitful lives.

> *Who is like the wise person,
> and who knows the explanation of things?*

> *Wisdom illumines the face*
> *and transforms a grim countenance.*

(Ecclesiastes 8:1)

Growing in wisdom gives us a better sense of the big picture; we grow to view things more as God desires. It's being able to view from the hilltop; to look at our lives and our world more as God does. Keep returning to our God, asking for his wisdom, growing closer to Him, experiencing and knowing his love, and then going out and sharing his love.

Day by Day

On the path of enhancing our discernment of God's will, St. Paul encourages us to pray continually, saying,

> *"With all prayer and supplication, pray at every opportunity in the Spirit."*

(Ephesians 6: 18)

Some of you may be thinking, "Ok, Deacon David, when it comes to nurturing my spiritual practices, I've dedicated myself to morning and evening prayer time, and I can even see myself offering intentions for the work or activities I do throughout my day, but to "pray at every opportunity in the Spirit"; I don't even know where to start or what that looks like."

Here's a thought. Ask yourself; when reflecting on how best to nurture my spiritual practices, perhaps I could look at activities (read opportunities) I am already practicing, that I find peace in, but I don't consider them spiritual practices? How might I already be involved in activities that make me feel more whole, or bring me closer to people, but I've yet to realize that these activities (these opportunities) can indeed be spiritual and bring me closer to God?

Gardening, cooking, playing the piano or guitar, baking, writing or reading, taking long walks or jogging, tinkering on an old car or motorcycle; anything that brings me peace. These are times to recognize the Holy Spirit's presence. Usually done alone, but it could be sharing time with that one friend that brings you to a holier place, or sharing a meal with your spouse, maybe it's bathing your little baby, or laying on the couch with your puppy gently petting him. In these areas and more, if it brings you peace, that's a good time to sense God's presence and recognize this moment He is giving you could be a beautiful moment for discernment.

Whatever the prayer, whatever the practice, as both grow you are being led closer to God and His presence. In the praying and in the doing you will find yourself hearing God's voice. As you increase your prayer time, as you gain in God's wisdom, and as you recognize the Holy Spirit more and more in your daily activities, you will come to realize who you truly are—you are a beloved child of God.

Key Takeaways

- **Can I carve ten minutes out of my mornings and evenings to spend in prayer?** This could be a short prayer, a moment of silence, or reading a passage of Scripture. Commit to these ten minutes; as you grow more comfortable, allow that time to increase.

- **How easy or difficult is it for me to sit in silence? Why might that be?** Initially I found sitting in silence difficult. If you find it difficult, my advice is to start with short periods, perhaps 2-3 minutes, and see if it grows. You might start by focusing on your breath or repeating a simple prayer or mantra like, "Come Holy Spirit."

- **What reservations might I have in asking God for His wisdom? How might I better address those reservations?** Understand that God is generous and will provide wisdom to those who seek it with a sincere heart. Acknowledge any reservations you might have and bring them to God in prayer.

- **Are there activities I enjoy that I could invite the Holy Spirit to join me; activities that could become spiritual practices where I might be able to discern God's will?** Think about activities you enjoy—and ask yourself, "How can I invite God into these moments?"

Chapter 9:

In Times of Uncertainty

Time in Prison...Time in Darkness

At my parish, St. Rose of Lima, in Houston, Texas, we have an active Kolbe Prison Ministry team. I've had the privilege of attending several Kolbe prison retreats, where inmates and men from the parish gather together to reflect on faith. For me, the most beautiful part of the retreat is hearing the inside team members' faith sharings and watching the impact it has on the other participants. It's a beautiful ministry and is a wonderful way to answer Jesus's call to visit the imprisoned; I encourage you to check out Kolbe Prison Ministries.

Visiting with Mike on day three of a Kolbe Prison ministry retreat in a maximum-security prison, he shared his story with me. We had gotten to know each other over the past three days when he finally felt comfortable enough to open-up.

Mike shared with me how he had been in prison for the past 18 years, and what his day-to-day life was like, the jobs he had done in prison, the educational courses he had completed, and his involvement with the Church. After hearing about his life, I said something to the effect of, "Well it's good to know that you keep yourself busy; that you're involved with the Church, that you have true friends here." Mike, slightly raising the palm of his hand and making a push-back gesture, looked me in my eyes and said, "With my sentence, I will never get out of here...I'm going to die here."...silence.

He went on to tell me the story of his life before prison,

how he married the girl of his dreams, and they had a baby boy. Unfortunately, their marriage did not prosper, drugs and alcohol being involved, until one day she took their son and left him.

Mike said that he spent the next three years trying to gain custody of his son, Luke, and finally due to his ex-wife's lifestyle, the court granted him full custody. The expression on his face as he reminisced this time in his life: pure bliss. His face remained lit up as he continued his story; sharing with me how he and Luke moved to another city where he found a good job and a good school for his son.

But next, his smile left as quickly as it had appeared, his face grew dour, tears welled in his eyes, and Mike then said, "My boy died a year later."

"I'm so sorry, Mike."

"It's ok, I know," and as his eyes found mine, Mike then said, "I went into a very dark place after Luke died…it's why I'm here."

Taking part in several Kolbe Prison Retreats, I've made a few friends along the way. Many have stories like Mike's; many came from violent or broken homes, grew up with no father figure, next drugs and alcohol came into play, and then a bad decision was made – leading each of these men to their own trials of darkness.

Ministering to men like Mike, and to be honest, allowing them to minister to me, I have been blessed to learn incredible lessons about our dark and light times, the hills and valleys we all go through in life. They've taught me much about prayer and faith. After hearing them share the long and difficult journeys they've been on, it's inspiring to witness how they've persevered through their darkest moments and emerged with a newfound sense of purpose and hope. Stories like this one:

What I want you to know is this. When I got to prison, it was the loneliest I've ever been; scared and lonely I turned to God and yelled at him...cussed at him...told him I hated him. And my actions that I had done that got me in here...I would think about those and further my hate for God. It was His fault that I was in this place.

For so long that darkness was just where I thought I was supposed to be and would be there forever, and I was ok with that...the anger in a weird way gave me a reason to go on...To live a life of hate is just who I figured I was...and honestly, I no longer cared...I just did not care. So, I continued hating God, blaming him...but then something happened...

One of the guys invited me to mass, figuring it was another way to get out of my cell for an hour, I said yes. I'm sitting in mass observing guys as they go up to receive the Eucharist and wondering why such reverence...why such a big deal over a little cracker?

The next week I went back to mass...and the next week and the next week. Before I knew it, I was taking RCIA classes...and I slowly came to the realization...God was with me...not against me. I now stand before you a baptized Catholic!

When I reflect on my conversion, I think strangely enough that in "hating" God I was still acknowledging him...I was still talking to him...I guess you could call it prayer...but it didn't at all feel like "prayer." God never left me...God was the only person who never left me...and when I realized that...good things started happening...even in a place like this...my anger subsided...I began to look at my brothers in here in a whole new way...my fear and anxieties began to turn to strength and trust in God...Instead of asking God, 'Why?' I began asking God, 'What am I supposed to do in here?' And slowly God answered...trust in me.'

> *Do not fear: I am with you;*
> *do not be anxious: I am your God.*
> *I will strengthen you, I will help you,*
> *I will uphold you with my victorious right hand."*
>
> (Isaiah 42:10)

Sitting in that prison gym listening to these stories and I am in tears. To hear a man who has been in prison for 20 years, and who knows he will never leave prison, who has been through things that most of us cannot imagine, stand up in front of 70 other inmates and share his story; the Holy Spirit is at work.

In concluding his sharing, he then said:

This is now my calling...to bring brothers who are where I used to be back to the Church...to bring my brothers back to God.

This inmate, this man, this beloved son of God, is truly at peace with himself; he understands discernment, he knows the love of Christ, he knows that he has been forgiven, and he knows what God wants and needs him to now go and do. I am in awe.

I tell this story of Mike and the other inmates as beautiful examples of patience and humility in surrendering to God. That even in the darkest of places, from some terrible act or experience, clinging to their own self-defeating willfulness and kicking and screaming along the way, these men finally found a way to surrender to God's will. From resentment and distrust to allowing God to hold them and then guide them, they found an upward path out of the darkness of the valley and into the light. When we find ourselves in a darkness that seems will never end, may their stories inspire us.

Patience and Humility

Nobody wants pain, or hurt, or illness, or hardships. This is life and life has its peaks and valleys; none of us are immune from times of darkness. Whether these events are brief or stretch on for weeks, months, or even years, they can shake our faith and make prayer feel like a struggle. Please remember, it's okay to yell, it's okay to ask why, it's okay to feel confused, and it's okay to be angry. Whatever the emotion, whatever the pain, bring it to Him…Cry out to Jesus.

Jesus Himself experienced deep sorrow, and we can often relate to Him the most in these moments. At the death of His friend Lazarus, Jesus wept and called out to His Father. (John 11:35, 41-42) There will be times when all we can do is sit with God and weep. In those times when we sit and weep, even uncontrollably, we are lamenting, and in the spiritual life it is in lamenting that we can then experience healing, hope and transformation. It is through lamenting that we are once again brought back into the light.

During times of darkness, when we're walking through the valley and when the path seems unclear. When we may wonder where God is in all of this, and as difficult as the situation seems, we must continue praying. We must continue asking for and bringing patience, humility, and honesty to our visits with God. And we must remember what Jesus taught us:

> *Blessed are they who mourn, for they will be comforted.*

(Matthew 5:4)

Discerning Saints Trying Times

Let nothing disturb you. Let nothing frighten you. Though all things pass, God does not change. Patience wins all things. But he lacks nothing who possesses God; for God alone suffices. [1] - St. Teresa of Avila

For her writing and teaching on prayer, St. Teresa of Avila, along with St. Catherine of Siena, were the first women honored with the title, Doctor of the Church. Throughout her life Teresa experienced many times of darkness. From losing her mother at a young age to bearing several serious illnesses to a period of several years after a major illness where she found it almost impossible to pray, Teresa struggled in her ongoing conversion, persevered and found her way back to a complete and whole life of prayer. Through all the difficulties and trials Teresa bravely endured, she held on to her faith, led the Carmelites, and founded several monasteries.

Teresa was a fearless woman who knew God, who listened to God, who knew what God wanted from her, and who inspired others to live a life for God. She was not afraid to share her personal spiritual life with others, and her writings, especially *The Way of Perfection* and *The Interior Castle,* have helped many in their personal spiritual journeys.

> *True, I am in love with suffering, but I do not know if I deserve the honor.* [2] -St. Ignatius of Loyola

Known for his dissolute lifestyle as a young nobleman, indulging in pleasure and excess, Ignatius of Loyola served as a commander in the Spanish army. He was gravely injured by a cannonball attack. What followed was a long road of torment, depression and pain; years in recovery during which he read, prayed, and discerned a call to religious life. Throughout his discernment, Ignatius kept his thoughts in a journal which ultimately became a series of meditations and spiritual exercises. These Spiritual Exercises of St. Ignatius, and the silent retreats that have stemmed from them, have helped many people for hundreds of years in their spiritual journeys and in discerning God's call.

Ignatius went on to form the Society of Jesus sending missions across Europe opening schools, colleges and seminaries. Today the Jesuits make up the largest male religious order in the Catholic Church comprising 28 colleges and universities and dozens of primary and high schools. And on March 13, 2013, our Church elected her first Jesuit leader: Pope Francis. All of this, because a once-time socialite who enjoyed gambling and pursuing young ladies, experienced a tragedy, turned to God, and slowly experienced a profound conversion, a wholehearted discernment that many would agree changed the world.

It's been said before that in times of trials, in those dark times when our faith may be tested, when we are hurting, it is in these times that we come closest to the suffering Jesus himself endured for our salvation. It is in these times that God perhaps does some of his best work…if we allow him.

These two saints, St. Teresa and St. Ignatius, and so many more, came to realize this in their own lives. They truly turned to God, discerned His calling, and patiently waited for his response. We should look to them as examples to follow.

> *...but we even boast of our afflictions, knowing that affliction produces endurance, and endurance, proven character, and proven character, hope, and hope does not disappoint, because the love of God has been poured out into our hearts through the holy Spirit that has been given to us.*
>
> (Romans 5: 3-5)

The saints show us, when we discern God's will, He appears to initially respond at a slow pace, allowing us to grow with Him and in Him, giving us just what we can handle, step by step. As we continue in faithful discernment, remaining faithful and continuing our walk with God hand-in-hand, God seems to show us more. And as He shows us more, He asks us for more. In the end, it does seem that God likes to go big!

Here are some tangible steps to stay rooted in prayer and discernment during challenging moments:

- **Start with honesty in prayer**: When you're struggling, don't shy away from telling God exactly how you feel. Bring your raw emotions to Him, whether angry, frustrated, or lost. It's not about having the perfect prayer—it's about showing up authentically. God can handle your questions, doubts, anger and pain.

- **Practice patience**: In times of uncertainty, trust that God's timing is perfect. It may feel like walking through a long, dark tunnel, but keep pressing forward. You may not see the light yet, but remember that spiritual growth often happens in the waiting. God is refining you for something greater.

- **Reflect on scripture**: Turn to passages that speak to God's faithfulness and promises in difficult times. Let the words of scripture anchor your heart as you walk through your valley.

- **Seek community and support**: You do not need to navigate these dark times alone. Contact trusted friends, family, or spiritual mentors who can support you in prayer and offer encouragement. Just as the inmates I've met in prison retreats supported each other, we, too, need others to help us grow in faith during tough times.

- **Ask for clarity and trust in God's will**: Trust that He is with you and guiding you. Be patient and open, knowing that discernment is a process that often unfolds over time.

Key Takeaways

- **Reflecting on Moments of Darkness:** Can I recall a time in my life when I felt as if I were walking in the valley? What did I feel? Did I feel God's presence? And if I made it out of the Valley, was God there with me? How did I then feel?

- **Turning to God in Tough Times:** When life gets tough, do I naturally turn to God, or do I turn away? Why?

- **Preparing to Discern God's Will in Uncertainty:** How can I prepare to continue discerning God's will, especially when facing hardship or uncertainty?

- **The Role of Patience and Humility in Discernment:** How might I bring more patience and humility to my prayer time and in discerning what God wants me to do?

References:
[1] Prayer of Saint Teresa of Avila, Eternal Word Television Network, *Prayers of the Saints*
[2] St. Ignatius of Loyola, Eternal Word Television Network, *Ignatius to the Trallians*

Chapter 10:

Spiritual Direction and Discernment

If you've made it to this chapter, I hope you've had a chance to reflect on your prayer life and journey of discernment. Perhaps you've realized that discernment is more than making decisions—it's an ongoing spiritual journey. It's about understanding God's will, which requires patience, humility, and a willingness to listen.

You may have spent time in prayer, inviting the Holy Spirit into your life in new ways, or perhaps you've started incorporating scripture into your daily moments with God. Maybe you've found a quiet place to sit and listen for God's whisper, or you've been more mindful of His presence as you go about your day. Some of you may have noticed small changes: a little more peace, a new openness to God's love, or moments in the day where you feel this new presence. Still, for others, they may be in a different place, with peace seemingly harder to find. Maybe that's you today. Things may not feel so good today as you may find yourself facing obstacles, challenges or difficulties. Please know that you are not alone. We all face seasons where our relationship with God feels distant, or we find it hard to pray. Yet, through all the seasons of our lives—whether walking through dark valleys or basking in the light—we share one constant: a longing to grow closer to God.

What I Hear You Saying is...

Whether you're just starting your spiritual journey, feeling lost and unsure of where to begin, or you've been practicing your faith for years, we all share a common need: the need for companionship on the path to holiness. Seeking the Lord is not a solitary journey; we need each other and companions who can help us grow and walk alongside us as we discern God's will for our lives. For many of us, I would say most of us, a spiritual director is one of the most valuable companions we can have on this journey.

When I first began meeting with my spiritual director, I felt nervous. I wasn't sure what to expect, and it took a few sessions before I felt comfortable enough to open up. But over time, I realized that her role wasn't to solve my problems or judge me. Instead, she sat with me in prayer, invited the Holy Spirit to be present, and listened attentively to what I was saying. She wasn't answering or telling me what to do; she was helping me listen for and to God. She often helped me understand what God might be saying to me, how He was working in my life, and in my discernment.

She may have been my "spiritual director," but she made it clear to me from the beginning who the real spiritual director was— the Holy Spirit. Her guidance was not her own, it was through the Holy Spirit that true discernment and wisdom were offered. This shift in perspective was intriguing to me; it reminded me that discernment is not about finding someone else's answer to my problems but about learning to listen to God's voice within me.

Spiritual direction is more than just a conversation—it's an opportunity for true growth. It's a chance to better our relationship with God, improve our lives, and impact the lives of those around us. During our sessions, when my spiritual director would say, "What I hear you saying is…" and I could respond with a heartfelt "Yes, that's it, thank you!" I knew the Holy Spirit was at work, guiding both of us. These moments of clarity became sacred.

Each time I left a session with my spiritual director, I felt a renewed peace. Yes, I still struggled with things, but the clarity I gained through our time together allowed me to approach my prayer life with new perspectives. My troubles didn't vanish, but I was better able to bring them to God, knowing that I had the tools to listen for His guidance. Over time, my prayer life grew richer, and I became more attuned to God's presence. Spiritual direction has been a crucial part of that growth. It has helped me navigate difficult moments, deepen my relationship with God, and, most importantly, better taught me how to hear His voice amid my questions and struggles. My prayer life is growing.

If you haven't yet experienced the benefits of spiritual direction, I encourage you to consider it. Whether you're struggling with direction in life, experiencing challenges in prayer, or simply seeking a deeper relationship with God, a spiritual director can help you better understand the movements of the Holy Spirit in your life; thus, helping you to draw closer to God.

Pope Francis on Spiritual Accompaniment

Pope Francis emphasizes the importance of spiritual direction, or as he prefers to call it, "spiritual accompaniment." He believes that the role of the spiritual accompaniment (or director) is not to take the place of God but to walk alongside you, helping you discern God's voice in your heart and in your life. In a General Audience, Pope Francis said:

> *He or she who accompanies does not substitute the Lord, does not do the work in the place of the person accompanied, but walks alongside him or her, encouraging them to interpret what is stirring in their heart, the quintessential place where the Lord speaks. The spiritual accompanier, whom we call spiritual director – I don't like this term, I prefer spiritual accompanier, it is better – they say: "Fine, but look here, look here", they draw your attention to things that perhaps pass you by; they help you understand better the signs of the times, the voice of the Lord, the voice of the tempter, the voice of the difficulties that you are unable to overcome. Therefore, it is very important not to journey alone. There is a wise African saying – because they have that tribal mysticism – which says: "If you want to arrive quickly, go alone; if you want to arrive safely, go with others", go in company, go with your people. This is important. In the spiritual life it is better to be accompanied by*

someone who knows about us and helps us. And this is spiritual accompaniment. [1]

Pope Francis reminds us that throughout the Gospels, we see Jesus connecting with people who trusted Him and with companions followed Him. Similarly, by regularly meeting with a trusted spiritual director, we can better discern God's will for our lives and recognize how His love is at work within us.

Finding a Spiritual Director

Finding a spiritual director may not always be easy, but it can be a positive step in deepening your spiritual journey. A spiritual director can provide guidance, offer insights into your discernment process, and help you better understand God's will for your life. When searching for one, here are some key things to keep in mind:

- **Look for Proper Training and Formation**: A good spiritual director should not only be trained but also have a deep formation in the practice of spiritual direction. Spiritual direction isn't just about offering advice; it's about listening carefully, discerning with you, and guiding you in your relationship with God. Look for someone who has studied spiritual direction formally and has experience guiding others.

- **Consider Established Programs**: There are well-established spiritual direction programs and schools that equip directors with the tools needed to guide others effectively. For example, the **Our Lady of Divine Providence School of Spiritual Direction** and **Marian Servants** offer trained directors across the United States, with many available in parishes. Other respected programs include **The Apostles of the Interior Life** and **The Lanteri Center for Ignatian Spirituality**.

- **Find a Good Personal Fit**: Spiritual direction is a deeply personal process. You will want a director who listens well, respects your pace, and fosters an atmosphere of trust. If you're unsure, consider having an initial meeting with a potential director to see if you feel comfortable with their approach and demeanor. You might need to meet with several people before you find someone who feels right for your journey.

- **Seek Recommendations**: Ask your parish priest, deacon, or trusted spiritual companions for recommendations. Many parishes offer spiritual direction through staff members who are well-formed and trained. Sometimes the right director may already be available within your own faith community.

- **Lay or Clerical Directors**: Many might think that a priest, or perhaps a deacon would make a good spiritual director, and not to offend any of our devoted priests or my brother deacons, but this is not always the case. Pope Francis has said that lay spiritual directors may have the gifted charism in spiritual direction. Spiritual direction is not a clerical charism, but rather a baptismal charism. He goes on to say that yes there are priests who have this charism, but it is not because they are priests; it is because they have been baptized. The baptized lay spiritual director may bring a secular wisdom to the seeker, which may be of great benefit in their discernment. [2]

- **Trust in the Process**: Finding the right spiritual director may take time, and the process is part of your spiritual journey. Trust that God will guide you to the right person who can help you deepen your relationship with Him and move forward in your discernment.

By taking the time to carefully choose a spiritual director, you might embark on a wonderful journey that will enrich your faith and help you navigate the complexities of discerning God's will for your life.

Balancing Discernment with Guidance

A good spiritual director functions like a trusted guide or a fellow traveler on the road of discernment, but they don't make the journey for you. Instead, they are there to walk alongside you, listening attentively, helping you process your thoughts and feelings, and always pointing you back to God. They offer tools to deepen your relationship with God—new ways to read scripture, different types of prayer, or methods to reflect on your life in a way that opens the door to hearing God's voice. Ultimately, the decision-making and discerning are still yours to make with God. The spiritual director can offer wisdom, but it's in your connection with God through prayer that true discernment happens. The process will take time, but trust in the journey, and allow your spiritual director to walk with you through the twists and turns of your discernment, helping you to stay focused on the voice of the One who truly knows you and calls you by name.

Continue to follow the guidance of your spiritual director and remain dedicated to discerning God's will. Through this process, you will grow in your belief that you are a beloved child of God, and your heart will become more aligned with His. As you move forward, you will discover the unique gifts, or charisms, that God has given you. Let these gifts guide you and make it your life's purpose to use them to fulfill the mission God created you for. Keep walking in faith, using your talents to serve others, and living in accordance with God's plan for your life.

Key Takeaways

- **Assess Your Prayer Life:**
  Where do you find yourself in your prayer life today? Reflect on whether you feel closer to God and identify any obstacles hindering your connection.

- **Reflect on Past Moments:**
  Think about how your "mountain-top" experiences and "valley" moments have shaped your prayer life. Have times of joy or hardship affected your commitment to prayer? How so?

- **Consider Companionship:**
  Have you relied on others, such as family, friends, or church groups, to support your spiritual life? Reflect on the impact of having companions on your journey. If you haven't had this support, think about reaching out to someone or joining a small group to walk alongside you in faith.

- **Explore Spiritual Direction:**
  Consider how a spiritual director might help guide your journey. Are there any specific areas of your

prayer life or spiritual journey where a spiritual director might be able to help you?

References:

[1] Pope Francis, *General Audience,* Paul VI Audience Hall, January 4, 2023

[2] Javier Garcia, *Pope explains that the laity can carry out spiritual direction of others*, Omnes Magazine, October 27, 2022

Chapter 11:

Discernment in Vocational and Life Choices

Life is full of decisions that can bring beauty and excitement. When a couple says, "We're talking about getting married," or a young man shares, "I'm thinking about going into the seminary," or a married couple says, "We want to have a baby," these decisions are often preceded by love, awe, and a sense of wonder. Such choices tend to bring joy, as they stem from a place of shared dreams and deep connection. A man and woman fall in love and decide to marry. A young man feels a gentle tug, a call to discern God's will in considering seminary. A married couple is certain in their hearts that they want to start a family together. These decisions and others like them fill us with joy and can produce beautiful memories.

Other major life decisions bring more difficulties or uncertainty. Someone may feel stuck in their current job and think, "I've got to leave this job and follow my passion, but I'm not sure how to make it happen." A new job opportunity has been offered, and one may sit and ask themselves, " I've been offered a new position with more time-consuming responsibilities but a higher salary, do I really want the position?" Still other life decisions may bring confusion, vulnerability, or pain, as one may unexpectedly find themselves alone and asking, "My spouse just told me they are leaving me, what am I now supposed to do?"

Whether in moments of joy, uncertainty, or pain, when facing major life decisions, we can easily turn to our egos and focus on the outcome of the decision. Our defenses rise and we quickly ask ourselves, "What do I think I should do? Is this the right decision for me? Is this what I want?" These questions we might ask ourselves, though natural, can sometimes overshadow the deeper reflection needed. We can become so caught up in the moment that we neglect to turn to God, sit with Him, ask for His guidance and discern His will.

Have You Brought it to Prayer?

Early in my diaconate formation, I can't count how many times my spiritual director would ask me, "Have you brought this to prayer?" whenever I shared a decision I was struggling with. Now, as a deacon, it's not uncommon for me to sit with someone facing a difficult decision and hear them express how much they're wrestling with it.

Sitting on a bench outside of the church one evening and visiting Kyle, who I was assisting with an annulment as his sponsor, he shared with me how difficult of a decision it had been to go forward with the annulment process. I asked him how much time he had spent in prayer on the decision. His response struck me, and I could completely relate when he said, "Deacon David, I really don't know how to pray about this."

> *In the same way, the Spirit too comes to the aid of our weakness; for we do not know how to pray as we ought, but the Spirit itself intercedes with inexpressible groanings. And the one who searches*

> *hearts knows what is the intention of the Spirit, because it intercedes for the holy ones according to God's will.*
>
> (Romans 8: 26-27)

"Kyle, rely on the Holy Spirit to help you, to intercede for you, to ask for you. There's two parts to prayer, we privately offer our petitions to God; we ask things, we tell him how we are doing and how we feel, what we are going through, and decisions we are struggling with. This is just the beginning of prayer. Then, we must wait, trusting that God will respond. And in God's reply you will get an answer, the answer may not always be immediate, straightforward, or what you expect. It may sound more like this: "Follow me…commit to letting go of all your fears, letting go of all your anxieties, letting go of your ego...trust in me."

Our prayer life is a journey, and in our discernment, as the stage is set and the curtain rises, in this holy and spiritual play of prayer, you may feel like the lead actor in Act 1 as you speak directly to God. But you must stay for Act 2. For it is in Act 2 when you realize that God has taken over, that he has the true leading role. And in knowing and allowing God to take the lead, you have come to understand that you are being guided, and led, and loved. And it is only then that you can, in true discernment ask:

Open the eyes of my heart, Lord.

Will this decision help me to continue to follow you Jesus?

God, with this decision, am I truly being the person you have made me to be?

Notice that these questions consider the path I am on with God. They are not a means to an end; they recognize a living continuation. They're not about choosing what I may think is best for me, but about recognizing that in every decision, what matters most is staying on the path with God, listening to His voice, and allowing Him to guide me in the right direction. It is not at all about arrival. It is a devotion to becoming the person that God made me to be.

The beauty of living a life of discernment is that as I grow closer in my relationship with God, I become more confident that I am on the journey He desires. My heart aligns more with His, and I worry less about making mistakes. I have finally realized that discernment is a process, not a decision. In *The Naked Now*, Richard Rohr beautifully writes that as our prayer life grows,

> *"God becomes more of a verb than a noun, more of a process than a conclusion, more of an experience than a dogma, more a personal relationship than an idea. There is someone dancing with you, and you are not afraid of making mistakes."* [1]

Come and Follow Me

Imagine the freedom we could experience if we truly embraced a life of discernment, following Jesus with all our hearts. I think about when the apostles first met Jesus—the pull they felt, the wonder and awe that must have filled them, and the deep love they experienced from Him.

> *"Come after me, and I will make you fishers of men" ...and at once Peter and Andrew, "left their nets and followed him." (Matthew 4:19-20)...As Jesus passed on from there, he saw a man named Matthew sitting at the customs post. He said to him, 'Follow me.' And he got up and followed him."*
>
> (Matthew 9:9)

In listening to Him and what He had to say, in hearing the good news of the kingdom of God, these apostles didn't just hear words—they felt His profound love. Then to have Jesus look into each of their eyes and say, "Follow me," imagine their experience. The love they felt was undeniable, transformative, and it stirred something deep within them.

In receiving Jesus' love, these apostles were faced with life-altering decisions. Drawn by His love, they chose to leave everything they had built their lives around. The fishermen left their nets and boats, their families' way of life. Matthew, the tax collector, walked away from the comfort and wealth of his position. These were not just decisions but acts of surrender, born from a deep sense of beauty, goodness, trust and love. Their ultimate life changing decisions to follow Jesus, rooted in divine love and discernment, changed their lives…their ultimate decisions to follow Jesus changed the world.

A Life Changed

I have a friend named Bart, a highly driven man. He quickly ascended the corporate ladder in the advertising and media industry, rising from director to executive roles and eventually making it to the C-suite.

One day, over lunch, Bart shared his story with me. He began, "I focused so much on success, hard work, and achievement. I threw myself entirely into these pursuits, believing that this relentless drive for accomplishment held all the answers I sought. But as I reached new heights, gaining influence, financial security, and success, I found none truly filled my emptiness. The things I thought would bring fulfillment only amplified the sense that something much deeper was missing."

Despite all of his success, Bart felt something was still lacking, an emptiness that wouldn't go away. Then he experienced a life-changing event, and Bart found himself at a crossroads. "When I became a father, everything shifted. I had a choice: I could teach my children the same lessons that shaped my path; hard work, success, and influence, or help them build something far more meaningful. I realized that the pursuit of worldly achievements wouldn't be enough. At some point, my children would face challenges that no amount of success or wealth could resolve."

Bart started to understand the power of discernment rather than simply making decisions based on his career or worldly goals. "I realized I had to stop focusing solely on my career and began discerning God's true calling for my life and my family. This journey of discernment led me to an important truth: the greatest gift my wife and I could offer our children wasn't success—it was faith. God created each of us for a unique purpose that went beyond worldly achievement. We wanted our children to know that God is the ultimate source of fulfillment, peace, and purpose, and that foundation of faith would carry them much farther than any career milestone ever could."

Together with his wife, Bart and his family began their journey of discernment. They realized that simply telling their children about faith wasn't enough. They had to live it out. "God called my wife and me to journey alongside our children, to model surrender, faith, and reliance on His provision in a way they could witness. We wanted them to truly understand what it means to seek God's Kingdom first," Bart shared.

As we finished our lunch, I was struck by Bart's honesty and how he and his wife had made discernment a central part of their lives. They weren't just making decisions based on convenience or worldly goals—they were listening for God's voice, seeking His will in every step. Bart concluded, "Today, God is at the heart of every conversation in our family. He is the foundation of our home and the center of our lives. As our children grow, they experience the world, but we are raising them to understand that they are not defined by it. Their childhood is very different from mine. They are growing up with a sense of purpose and belonging because they know God."

Bart's story is a beautiful reminder of the importance of discerning God's will, especially during life-changing events. When we rely on our egos and worldly measures of success, we often find an emptiness that can't be filled. But when we let go of control, turn to God, and discern His path, we find the peace and fulfillment only He can provide. Bart is one of the most joyful people I know. His joy stems from living a purposeful life rooted in discernment and alignment with God's will.

As we journey through life, we are constantly faced with decisions—some small, others life-changing. The key to navigating these choices with clarity and peace lies in discernment. Discernment is not simply about making the "right" choice; it's about aligning our hearts and minds with God's will. It's about growing in relationship with

Him, trusting that He is guiding us through the Holy Spirit, and allowing His love to shape every decision we make.

Key Takeaways

- **Reflecting on Past Decisions: How Did You Involve God?** Think back to the last time you made a life-changing decision. Did you bring that decision to God? How did you bring God into your decision-making process? Knowing what you now know, how might have you differently brought your situation to God?

- **Relying on the Holy Spirit for Guidance:** How do you rely on the Holy Spirit in your prayer life? How might you grow in leaning in on the Holy Spirit, on trusting that the Holy Spirit is with you and within you to guide you in all of life's decisions?

- **Reflect on Matthew 9:9-13:** Read Matthew 9: 9-13. Imagine yourself sitting at the table with Jesus, Matthew, and the others. What might the Holy Spirit be sharing with you as you reflect on this passage?

- **Facing Life-Changing Decisions:** What life-changing decision might you be facing now or in the future? Consider how you can approach this decision with discernment and prayer. What would it feel like to truly let go of your ego and rely on God and His guidance, on His love

References:

[1] Richard Rohr, *The Naked Now: Learning to See as the Mystics See*, The Crossroad Publishing Company, (2009)

Chapter 12:

The Fruit of Discernment: A Life Aligned with God

In a recent conversation with our OCIA (Order of Christian Initiation of Adults) class about their discernment process into the Church and their prayer lives, Tim, one of our catechumens, asked me what the biggest lesson was that I took away from my time in diaconate formation. My response was:

> *"What I discovered was God wants me to just be David; the David he intended me to be...What I discovered was that discernment is a way of life...that it completes me...that I cannot live the life God made me to live without living a life of daily discernment...that it is very difficult to walk with Christ, to be a disciple of Christ, without living a life of daily discernment."*

-Deacon David Dufilho

As I became an adult, here is what discernment looked like for me. My first "big" discernment, my first life-changing discernment, was deciding to marry my beautiful wife. When we announced our engagement, some friends and family thought we were too young. Some thought our marriage wouldn't work out as we had only dated for 3 months. Both were wrong. Yira and I, with the assistance of our pastor, Fr. Richard, discerned for nine months, and both of us came to realize that God was in this with us and for us. Having understood God completes our marriage from the beginning, Yira and I recently celebrated our 32nd anniversary.

I've had a few other "life-changing" discernments; finishing my degree, having children, changing careers, deciding on what schools our boys would attend, but only one other true "life-changing" discernment comes close to my decision to get married, and that was my discerning the diaconate. Inquiry, Aspiration, and Candidacy: six years of formation and six years of coming to an understanding of discerning God's will have led me and guided me to this beautiful ministry of the diaconate.

Finally, and just as importantly, what I learned in diaconate formation and have tried to carry over in my day-to-day life is this ongoing daily discernment that flows from and through my two major life discernments. I try as I can, though many times difficult, to hear God's voice, to hear his call, and to see his works in my routine day-to-day life, in all of its ordinary experiences, and yes, praise God, sometimes extraordinary experiences.

Daily Discernment aligned with God

Speaking about his papacy and his daily discernment with God, I think Pope Francis summed it up best when he said:

Discernment is always done in the presence of the Lord, looking at the signs, listening to the things that happened, the feeling of the people, especially the poor. My choices, including those related to the day-to-day aspects of life, like the use of a modest car, are related to a spiritual discernment that responds to a need that arises from looking at things, at people, and from reading the signs of the times. Discernment in the Lord guides me in my way of governing. [1] -Pope Francis

Throughout the Gospels, Jesus emphasizes the importance of listening, hearing, and seeing if we are to truly follow Him and understand what He desires for us. This is the essence of daily discernment.

Jesus said:

> *Whoever has ears ought to hear.*
>
> (Matthew 11:15)
>
> *Do you have eyes and not see, ears and not hear?*
>
> (Mark 8:18)

Take care, then, how you hear.

(Luke 8:18)

I came into this world for judgment, so that those who do not see might see...

(John 9:39)

As I sit down at the end of my day, inviting the Holy Spirit to join me in reflecting on the day, I ask the Lord to guide me through the remembrance of my day, my thoughts and actions, my interactions with people, places, and nature—both positive and negative—that's key. Where, God, did you speak to me? What did you say? What do you want me to hear? What do you want me to see?

In daily asking the Lord of these things, what we are doing is asking for his guidance, and if we continue to do so, what will happen over time is that our asking and wanting will turn into a realization, a reliance on his guidance. We'll begin to see and hear Him more and more throughout our days; we'll see him in others, in nature, our communities, our work, and our play, in a sunrise and a sunset; we will hear and see. Just as the Pope says, *"Discernment in the Lord guides me in my way of governing,"* so too will our discernment guide us in our vocations, ministries, and callings.

As we continue to reflect on how the Holy Spirit inspires us from within and outside ourselves, looking at our relationships with our interior selves and our relationships with others, we will begin to know how to answer and then live God's call.

More Peace…More Purpose

> *The fruits of the Spirit are perfections that the Holy Spirit forms in us as the first fruits of eternal glory. The tradition of the Church lists twelve of them: charity, joy, peace, patience, kindness, goodness, generosity, gentleness, faithfulness, modesty, self-control, and chastity.*
>
> (CCC 1832)

Through baptism and confirmation, we are sealed with the Holy Spirit and gifted with the fruits of the Spirit. As Catholics, we are called to cooperate with and grow in these gifts, allowing the Holy Spirit to work in us and our lives as we seek to discern God's will.

So, what does living a life of discernment look like? What does it feel like? It's a life filled with peace and purpose, walking with God. This is the life that we all long for. St. Paul assures us that this life is attainable but doesn't come easily. Few people who lead purposeful lives would claim that it's easy. That's why, as Catholics, we've been given the seven gifts of the Holy Spirit—wisdom, understanding, knowledge, counsel, fortitude, piety, and fear of the Lord.

These gifts are there to assist us in living lives of discernment.

No saint lived an easy life, but each one lived a purposeful life—one that brought peace. St. Paul reminds us:

In doing so, we will experience *"the fruit of the Spirit,"* which includes *"love, joy, peace, patience, kindness, generosity, faithfulness, gentleness, self-control"*

(Galatians 5:22)

Living a life of discernment and purpose may not be comfortable, but it is meaningful. I don't believe God wants us to leave this earth well-rested. On the contrary, I believe He wants us to leave tired, ready to meet Him, knowing that we have sincerely tried to do everything He put us on this earth to do.

Key Takeaways

- **Life-Changing Events and Discernment:** Reflect on the significant life-changing events you've faced. How have you brought these decisions to God in discernment? What difference did that make in how you navigated those moments? Consider the peace or clarity you may have received through God's guidance.

- **Listening for God in Your Daily Life:** How can you better cultivate a habit of listening for God in your day-to-day life? Are there moments or places where you might be missing His voice? Try setting aside time each day, even just a few minutes, to quiet yourself and intentionally seek His presence.

- **Relying on the Gifts of the Holy Spirit:** How might you depend more on the gifts of the Holy Spirit—wisdom, understanding, counsel, and others—as you make decisions and navigate life? Reflect on how these gifts could shape your choices, relationships, and spiritual growth.

- **Desiring the Fruits of the Holy Spirit:** Which fruits of the Holy Spirit (love, joy, peace, patience, kindness, generosity, faithfulness, gentleness, and self-control) do you most desire today? Why? Consider specific areas in your life where these fruits could be most impactful. Pray and ask the Holy Spirit to cultivate these fruits within you.

References:

[1] Antonio Spadaro S.J., *A Big Heart Open to God: An interview with Pope Francis*, America The Jesuit Review, (September 20, 2013)

Chapter 13:

Discernment as a Daily Practice

> *Prayer presupposes an effort, a fight against ourselves and the wiles of the Tempter. The battle of prayer is inseparable from the necessary 'spiritual battle' to act habitually according to the Spirit of Christ: we pray as we live, because we live as we pray.*
>
> (CCC 2752)

The Way We Pray, is the Way We Believe, is the Way We Live

It was a new semester, still early in my diaconate formation, and I'm sitting at my desk, waiting for my first class, *Liturgy of the Mass*, to begin. The instructor walks in, looks up from his podium, and begins, "Lex Orandi, Lex Credendi, Lex Vivendi." These Latin words translate to, "The way we pray, is the way we believe, is the way we live." Every time we met for class that semester, Deacon Philip would begin by proclaiming, "Lex Orandi, Lex Credendi, Lex Vivendi," those words have stayed with me ever since, continuing to guide and shape my discernment today.

The Way We Pray

Early in this book, I suggested setting aside ten minutes each morning and evening for prayer. If you're just starting, this is a great way to begin your journey. However, this is just the beginning.

Later in Chapter 10, I shared my hope that you'll recognize your walk with Jesus more clearly as your prayer life develops. You might notice that things feel different—that by His grace, the recognition of a deep desire to grow closer to God does reside in you. Whether you have found that desire or not, wherever you are, always remember that our God is a patient God, and He'll wait, He'll never leave no matter where you are in your journey.

Remain faithful, continue your walk, and dedicate yourself to prayer time. Through your words and actions, offer prayers for others, seeking to recognize God's work in every part of your day. Keep nurturing your prayer life, knowing that every step forward brings you closer to Him.

The Way We Believe

Where do we go from here? How can we grow in our belief and strengthen our connection to God's will? What might be some practical advice for integrating more discernment into our everyday lives, making space, both physical and internal, for regular spiritual reflection and formation as we move to a life that continuously seeks God's will? Are there things we can do, or can stop doing, that might assist us in our discernments of God's will?

Ultimately, integrating discernment into our lives is about seeking God's will in both big and small decisions and committing to growing in our relationship with Him each day. By making space—both physically and mentally—for

God's presence and being intentional about our habits, we will begin to notice more clearly how He is leading us, moment by moment.

The Way We Live

What did you do yesterday? Maybe you went to work, hit the gym, had lunch with a client, started a new project, or quickly left the office to get your son to baseball practice on time. All of these are good things, meaningful activities, and for most of us, our days are filled with such responsibilities, especially when it comes to caring for our families. These are holy and noble tasks. But could there be activities or moments in my day that I could reconsider?

Committing to a life that continually seeks God's will begins with looking honestly at myself and how I spend my days. As the saying goes, hindsight is 20/20, and reflecting on the past can provide valuable insight for moving forward on this journey of discernment. So, let's pause and take inventory of how we spend our time.

Ask yourself: How much time have I devoted to my prayer life? Could I carve out more time to spend with God? How have I intentionally shaped my day to align with seeking and doing God's will? Next, ask the more challenging questions:

- What activities occupy my time that I should perhaps reconsider?

- What kind of music am I listening to?
- What books am I reading?
- What TV shows am I watching?
- What podcasts am I listening to?
- What language do I use or allow others to use around me?

Now, reflect on these activities. Do they bring me closer to God or push me away from Him?

Here's the reality we may need to face:

- Prayer will be much more difficult if I've spent the past two hours sitting in front of the TV watching people argue about left or right issues.
- Prayer will be much more difficult if I listen to certain podcasts…you know the ones.
- Prayer will be much more difficult if I've spent the past two hours on Netflix watching an inappropriate movie.
- Prayer will be much more difficult if golf comes before Sunday mass.
- Prayer will be much more difficult if I do not participate in the sacraments, the Eucharist, and Reconciliation.

Entering prayer with a sincere, open heart can be difficult when we fill our lives with distractions that harden our hearts and inflate our egos. We must be honest with ourselves, reflecting on the choices we make in our daily routines. Candidly ask: Are the things I participate in bringing me closer to God, or are they pulling me away from Him?

> *So I declare and testify in the Lord that you must no longer live as the Gentiles do, in the futility of their minds; darkened in understanding, alienated from the life of God because of their ignorance, because of their hardness of heart,*
>
> (Ephesians 4: 17-18)

The Friends We Keep

Quick—who are your closest friends? Why do you consider them close?

Many self-help authors have written similar statements: "If you want to succeed, surround yourself with successful people." Or, one of my favorites: "Show me your friends, and I'll show you what kind of person you are."

So, I ask myself, What kind of company do I keep? Are the people around me helping me grow spiritually? And, more importantly, do I also help them on their journeys?

It is impossible to live a life that continually seeks God's will without living in communion with others. Our journey with God isn't a solo endeavor; it requires us to live for others in fellowship and connection. I go back to my daily challenging prayer: "Lord, help me to be Your light for others today and to see You in everyone I meet." It's a reminder that Jesus is present in the people around us and that we are called to be present for them, too.

Jesus didn't carry out His mission alone. He relied on the companionship of His twelve friends (Luke 9:1-2), and He longs to use and rely on you and me as branches of His vine (John 15:1- 5), to work together in fulfilling His will. Ultimately, our discernment is about playing our individual roles while joined together in bringing His kingdom to earth. *Thy kingdom come, Thy will be done on earth as it is in heaven.* We need each other. We need friendship.

So, where can we find and nurture these friendships? The most obvious place is in our parish. Whether it's becoming an extraordinary minister, or a reader, a sacristan or choir member, all of these, and many others, foster holiness. Volunteer at the food bank or help in leading a CCE class. Get involved with the Altar Guild or Men's Club; there's many future friendships just waiting, waiting to grow as we serve our parish and as we serve God. My parish has over sixty ministries, and participating in any of these ministries is the very act of discernment, as they join us in community, assist us in our discernment, and help us in living out God's will.

Being in a community plays a large role in seeking His will. Our gift to God is doing His will, His gift to us—new, closer, and holier friendships. In doing good with and for others, what we're doing, what we're growing, what we're advancing, what we're becoming, what we're building—God's kingdom here on earth.

Key Takeaways

- **How Does My Prayer Impact My Belief?** Reflect on how your prayer life shapes your beliefs. Are your prayers helping you grow closer to God? Do you notice a connection between your beliefs and how you live your life?

- **Are There Activities I Might Want to Reconsider?** Take a moment to examine your daily activities. Are there habits, hobbies, or routines that may not be aligned with the life you want to live in faith

- **Do I Support My Friends' Spiritual Journeys?** Think about the people in your life. Are you helping your friends in their spiritual walks? Are you a source of encouragement, support, and prayer for them? Also, reflect on whether your friends are helping you grow spiritually.

- **What Parish Ministries Am I Most Drawn To?** Explore the ministries at your parish and reflect on which ones resonate with you. Are there specific ministries or roles that you feel passionate about?

Chapter 14:

Living Out Discernment in Our World…In God's World

Keepers, Not Merely Seekers

The Christian life is fundamentally a life of discernment. Through prayer and daily reflection, empowered by the sacraments we cherish, we seek God's will for us in small moments and significant decisions. Doing so allows us to go out into the world, serve others, and fulfill God's mission. In living out His will, we become keepers, not merely seekers, of His love.

Always remember that God saved us by serving us. We may think that in discerning God's will we are serving Him, but we must first acknowledge that God is the one who first freely chose to serve us. He loved us first. It is difficult to love without being loved in return, and it's nearly impossible to serve others if we have not allowed ourselves to be served by God. We were born in love (God), to be loved (first by God), and to love (God and our neighbor).

In his Palm Sunday homily celebrating World Youth Day 2020, Pope Francis said,

Jesus says to each one of us, 'Courage, open your heart to my love'. You will feel the consolation of God who sustains you…We were put in this world to love him and our neighbors. Everything else passes away, only this remains.

And in his closing, pointing to all the doctors, nurses, emergency personnel, clergy, moms and dads, and so many others who got us through the pandemic, Pope Francis said:

Dear Friends, look at the real heroes who come to light in these days: they are not famous, rich and successful people; rather, they are those who are giving themselves in order to serve others. Feel called yourselves to put your lives on the line. Do not be afraid to devote your life to God and others; it pays! For life is a gift we receive only when we give ourselves away, and our deepest joy comes from saying yes to love, without ifs and buts. To truly say yes to love, without ifs and buts. As Jesus did for us. [1]

I'll Help You Carry Your Load…

Person by person, eye to eye, in living rooms, on street corners, and in front of small and large crowds, Peter, Paul, and the other apostles, along with the disciples who followed them, touched all as they preached and lived the gospel. They didn't preach from a distance—they shared the love of Jesus face-to-face with every individual they met. And once they shared the good news, they sent those new believers back to their ordinary lives to witness to others.

Person to person, knee to knee, eye to eye, a shoulder lent for a head, or a loving embrace, here is where the gospel was shared, here is where the Spirit was found. The same holds true today, and it holds true in our everyday interactions and in every type of work we do.

People who choose to live a life of discernment, whatever their occupation, whatever roles they play. From teachers to CEOs, from cooks to police officers, from nurses to news producers, and in every other line of dignified work; the way they do their work in graceful service to their students and employees, hungry customers and neighbors, patients and viewers, in their day-to-day ordinary lives, these followers of Jesus are advancing His kingdom. These folks, in their daily discernment with God know that their life is about relationship to God and relationship to one another. And in their daily witness of growing God's kingdom, each time their eyes meet another's, they see the face of Jesus, and they say, "I'm here to help you carry your load."

Live that life of discernment. Be that person, be that disciple of Jesus, be that beloved child of God…and play your role in advancing His kingdom.

Key Takeaways

How Do I Allow God to Serve Me? Reflect on how you invite God's love and grace into your life. Do you make space for Him to guide, heal, and fill you with peace? Consider how you can be more open to receiving God's service.

- **How Can I Serve God's Kingdom?** Think about the ways you can actively give of yourself to serve God's mission. Whether through work, family, community involvement, or personal acts of kindness, consider how to bring God's love to those around you.

- **Selfless Giving:** Reflect on when you gave selflessly to someone else. How did that act of service make you feel? Did you experience a sense of fulfillment, joy, or growth?

- **Bringing the Light of Christ to My Work:** Think about how you can bring Christ's love into your daily work. Whether you're interacting with coworkers, customers, or clients, how can you shine a light on your work and the people you serve?

References:

[1] Pope Francis, *Homily of His Holiness Pope Francis*, Celebration Of Palm Sunday Of The Passion Of The Lord, 35th World Youth Day, St. Peters Basilica, April 5, 2020

Epilogue:

An Invitation

I hope you've enjoyed *Discernment Not Decision*, and I invite you to continue this transformative journey with us. Our podcast, *Discernment, Not Decisions*, is available now, along with online courses and in-person workshops designed to deepen our understanding and practice of living a life of discernment.

Through the podcast, we will explore more insights into discerning God's will and how we can apply it in our daily lives. It's a great way to continue walking alongside others who are also seeking to live more intentional and discerning lives.

Our online courses and in-person workshops offer an opportunity to dive even deeper. They'll help you engage in practical exercises and discussions while growing together in and as a community of discerning disciples. You can join us now, with the podcast available wherever you listen, and explore the courses and workshops through our parish website at stroselima.org.

We're excited to continue this journey with you and look forward to walking alongside you as we grow in discernment.

And Finally

This entire book has been a discernment:

God, do you want me to write this book?

What do you want me to write?

What stories and experiences should I share?

Point me to the scripture verses I should reflect on and include.

Guide my heart...guide my mind...give me the words.

I pray that I remain in You, as I trust with my whole heart that You remain in me.

From the front cover to the back, the entire project of completing this book, the whole journey, and working with my wonderful team has been a blessing. That's what happens—we discern God's will...He leads us...He guides us...He loves us through it...He gifts us, and He blesses us. And we, in return, take His gift and gift it to others...we witness to them, and in our witness, we guide them...lead them...love them...always turning back to our Lord in prayer...

As Jesus sought the quiet of the desert,

teach us to pray.

As Jesus washed the feet of his disciples,

teach us to love.

As Jesus promised paradise to the thief on the cross,

teach us to hope.

As Jesus called Peter to walk to him across the water,
teach us to believe.

As the child Jesus sat among the elders in the temple,
teach us to seek answers.

As Jesus in the garden opened his mind and heart to God's will,
teach us to listen.

As Jesus reflected on the Law and the prophets,
teach us to learn.

As Jesus used parables to reveal the mysteries of the Kingdom,
teach us to teach. Amen

-Litany of the Way, Prayer for the Journey

So I end here where I began. Just as it was with Jesus' baptism, so it is with yours, a voice from heaven is whispering, "You are a beloved son. You are a beloved daughter and in you I am well pleased."

Listen to His voice…answer His call…begin your journey…

Discernment not Decisions
Reference Listing

Chapter 1

[1] Richard Rohr, *Discernment versus Decision Making*, Daily Meditations, Center for Action and Contemplation, May 31, 2018.
[2] Henri Nouwen, *Discernment: Reading the Signs of Daily Life* (Harper One: 2013), 17.
[3] Richard Rohr, *Discerning What is Ours to Do*, Daily Meditations, Center for Action and Contemplation, August 21, 2022.

Biblical References (NABRE)

Romans 12:2 - Sacrifice of Body and Mind
John 15:4-5 - The Vine and the Branches

Chapter 2

[1] St. John Chrysostom, *Ecloga de Oration* 2: 63,585
[2] Cindy Wooden, *Discernment is Essential to Discipleship, Papal Preacher Says*, CNS March 22, 2024

Biblical References (NABRE)

1 Kings 3:9-12 - Early Promise of Solomon's Reign
Proverbs 2:1-5 - The Blessings of Wisdom
Philippians 1:9-11 - Paul's Prayer for the Philippians

1 Corinthians 2:14-15 - The True Wisdom
1 Corinthians 3:1 - On Divisions in the Corinthian Church
Luke 2:48-49 - The Boy Jesus in the Temple
Luke 4:1-12 - The Temptation of Jesus
Mark 1:35 - Jesus Leaves Capernaum
Luke 6:12 - The Mission of the Twelve
Luke 9:28-29 - The Transfiguration of Jesus
Luke 21:37-38 - Ministry in Jerusalem
Matthew 26:36-46, Mark 14:32-42, Luke 22:39-46 - The Agony in the Garden
John 17:20-26 - The Prayer of Jesus
Matthew 7:15-18 - False Prophets

Catechism of the Catholic Church. 2nd ed. Vatican: Libreria Editrice Vaticana, 1994

CCC, 1809   The Cardinal Virtues
CCC, 1787   To Choose in Accord with Conscience

Chapter 3

Biblical References (NABRE)

Genesis 1:27 - The Story of Creation
Luke 11:9-10 - The Answer to Prayer

Catechism of the Catholic Church. 2nd ed. Vatican: Libreria Editrice Vaticana, 1994

CCC, 2563   Prayer as Covenant

Chapter 4

[1] Mother Teresa, *Do Something Beautiful For God, The Essential Teachings of Mother Teresa*, Blue Sparrow Publishing 2020, p. 40

Catechism of the Catholic Church. 2nd ed. Vatican: Libreria Editrice Vaticana, 1994

CCC, 2699	The Life of Prayer
CCC, 2700	Vocal Prayer
CCC, 2705-2706	Meditation
CCC, 2715	Contemplative Prayer
CCC, 2826	Thy Will be Done on Earth as it is in Heaven

Biblical References (NABRE)

Matthew 26:39 - The Agony in the Garden

Chapter 5

Catechism of the Catholic Church. 2nd ed. Vatican: Libreria Editrice Vaticana, 1994

CCC, 1936   Equality and Differences Among MenBiblical References

James 4:8 - Causes of Division
1 Thessalonians 5:17 - Church Order
Matthew 28:20 - The Commissioning of the Disciples
Matthew 18:20 - A Brother Who Sins

Genesis 2:18 - The Garden of Eden
1 Corinthians 13:4,6 - The Gift of Love

Chapter 6

[1] Ronald Rolheiser, Prayer: *Our Deepest Longing* (Franciscan Media, 2013), pp. 44-46
[2] Ronald Rolheiser, *Some Advice on Prayer from an Old Master*, www.ronrolheiser.com, May 31, 2020

Biblical References (NABRE)

Luke 8:11-15 - The Parable of the Sower Explained

Chapter 7

Biblical References (NABRE)

Matthew 17:5-8 - The Transfiguration of Jesus
2 Peter 1:5-8 - The Power of God's Promise

Chapter 8

Biblical References (NABRE)

Psalm 46:11 - God, the Protector of Zion
Matthew 7:24 - The Two Foundations
1 Corinthians 2:12-13 - The True Wisdom
James 1:5 - Perseverance in Trial
Ecclesiastes 8:1 - Critique of Advice to Heed Authority
Ephesians 6:18 - Constant Prayer

Chapter 9

[1] Prayer of Saint Teresa of Avila, *Prayers of the Saints*, Eternal Word Television Network
[2] St. Ignatius of Loyola, *Ignatius to the Trallians*, Eternal Word Television Network

Biblical References (NABRE)

Isaiah 41:10 - The Liberator of Israel
Matthew 5:4 - The Beatitudes
Psalm 23:4 - The Lord, Shepherd and Host
John 10:11 - The Good Shepherd
Romans 5:3-5 - Faith, Hope, and Love

Chapter 10

[1] Pope Francis, *General Audience,* Paul VI Audience Hall, January 4, 2023
[2] Javier Garcia, *Pope explains that the laity can carry out spiritual direction of others*, Omnes Magazine, October 27, 2022

Chapter 11

[1] Richard Rohr, *The Naked Now*, PublishDrive, September 1, 2009

Biblical References (NABRE)

Romans 8:26-27 - Destiny of Glory

Matthew 4:19-20 - The Call of the First Disciples
Mathew 9:9 - The Call of Matthew

Chapter 12

[1] Antonio Spadaro S.J., *A Big Heart Open to God: An interview with Pope Francis*, America The Jesuit Review, (September 20, 2013)

Catechism of the Catholic Church. 2nd ed. Vatican: Libreria Editrice Vaticana, 1994

CCC, 1832   The Gifts and Fruits of the Holy Spirit

Biblical References (NABRE)

Matthew 11:15 - Jesus' Testimony to John
Mark 8:18 - The Leaven of the Pharisees
Luke 8:18 - The Parable of the Lamp
John 9:39 - The Man Born Blind
Galatians 5:22-25 - Freedom for Service

Chapter 13

Catechism of the Catholic Church. 2nd ed. Vatican: Libreria Editrice Vaticana, 1994

CCC, 2752   The Prayer of the Hour of Jesus

Biblical References (NABRE)

Ephesians 4:17-18 - Renewal in Christ

Luke 9:1-2 - The Mission of the Twelve
John 15:1-5 - The Vine and the Branches

Chapter 14

[1] Pope Francis, *Homily of His Holiness Pope Francis, Celebration Of Palm Sunday Of The Passion Of The Lord*, 35th World Youth Day, St. Peters Basilica, April 5, 2020

About the Author

Deacon David Dufilho serves the St. Rose of Lima community in Houston Texas along with ministering to the sick at Hermann Memorial Hospital. Married for over 32 years to his wife Yira, they have two adult sons, Avery and Carter, and share their home with their much-loved bull terrier, Otis. Deacon David's favorite bible verse: "…so that they may all be one, as you, Father, are in me and I in you that they also may be in us…" (John 17:21)

About St. Rose of Lima Catholic Church

At St. Rose of Lima, located at 3600 Brinkman St, Houston, TX 77018, our mission is to create a welcoming community where everyone is invited to experience God's love and grace. We accomplish this by offering a place at the table of the Lord for all—whether lifelong parishioners, newcomers, or those in need. Through our ministries, outreach programs, and daily actions, we strive to embody Christ's love by serving others, fostering spiritual growth, and building meaningful connections.

We invite you to join us for Mass and become a part of our vibrant faith community. Visit us today at stroselima.org and come experience the love and warmth of St. Rose of Lima.

Made in the USA
Middletown, DE
14 April 2025

74244581R00106